Peter Cochrane

TOBRUK 1941

ABC
Books

In memory of George Silk
1916–2004
the last of the Tobruk photographers

 The ABC 'Wave' device is a trademark of the Australian
Broadcasting Corporation and is used under licence by
HarperCollinsPublishers Australia.

First published in Australia in 2002 by ABC Books
for the Australian Broadcasting Corporation
Reprinted by HarperCollinsPublishers Australia Pty Limited
ABN 36 009 913 517
harpercollins.com.au

HarperCollins*Publishers*
Level 13, 201 Elizabeth Street, Sydney NSW 2000, Australia
Unit D1, 63 Apollo Drive, Rosedale, Auckland 0632, New Zealand
A53, Sector 57, Noida, UP, India
77–85 Fulham Palace Road, London W6 8JB, United Kingdom
2 Bloor Street East, 20th floor, Toronto, Ontario M4W 1A8, Canada
10 East 53rd Street, New York NY 10022, USA

National Library of Australia Cataloguing-in-Publication entry:

Cochrane, Peter, 1950–
Tobruk 1941.
ISBN: 978 0 7333 1407 0.
1. Australia. Army. Division, 9th. 2. Tobruk, Battles of,
1941–1942 - Pictorial works. 3. World War, 1939–1945 - Campaigns.
I. Australian Broadcasting Corporation. II Title.
940.540994

Cover photographs (front) 005392 and (back) 020738
courtesy of the Australian War Memorial
Designed by Melanie Feddersen, i2i design
Colour reproduction by Pageset, Victoria
Printed and bound in Singapore by Tien Wah Press

8 7 6 5   14 15

There is to be no surrender and no retreat.

Lieutenant-General Leslie Morshead, Tobruk 1941

CONTENTS

TOBRUK

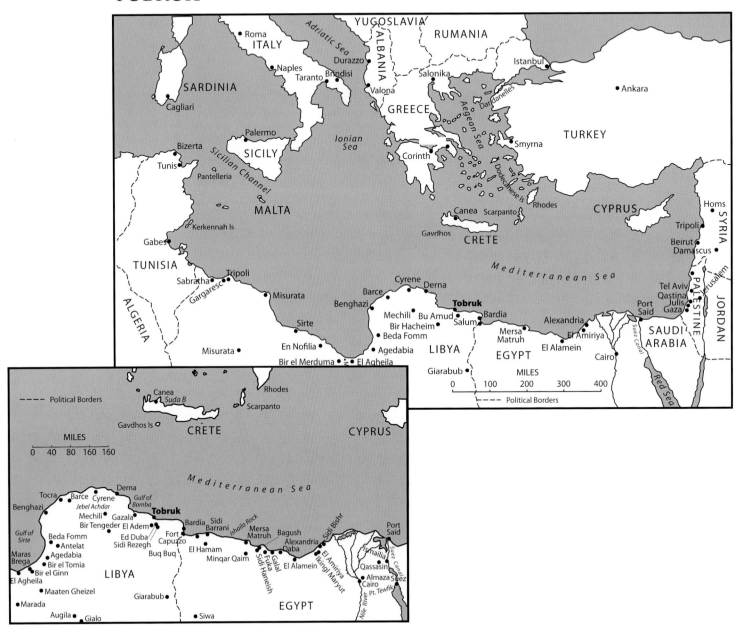

INTRODUCTION

There will be no Dunkirk here. If we should have to get out, we shall fight our way out. There is to be no surrender and no retreat.

Lieutenant-General Leslie Morshead, Tobruk 1941

When Italy entered the war in June 1940, Mussolini's garrison towns on the North African coast became a threat to the Allies. British control of Egypt and the Suez Canal was now imperilled by Italian forces to the west, in Il Duce's Libya. One of these garrison towns was Tobruk.

The town itself was little more than a cluster of stuccoed, flat-topped houses on the northern slopes of an ample harbour, the sameness of the buildings somewhat offset by the white-washed, concrete barracks of the military, the gun emplacements on the ridge tops, the naval establishment on the foreshore and the shipping on the water.

Tobruk was a sand-blown outpost on the edge of the Libyan Desert, a terminal recess where the heat, rats, flies, sand fleas and boredom turned all hope in the garrison in one direction – to escape – and all ambition rested on one word – repatriation. But Tobruk was destined to be a prize, to be fought for again and again in the next two years, with a ferocity that could only be explained by its strategic location and other military charms: it had a deep water harbour, a plentiful supply of subterranean drinking water and it was a 'fortress' of sorts. Tobruk was the only good harbour between Benghazi and Alexandria; it possessed the only good water supply between Derna and Mersa Matruh. No army could press on to Suez with Tobruk in the hands of the enemy, for that could mean an end to supply lines, encirclement and ruination.

The fortifications at Tobruk were embedded in a perimeter surrounding the town. The 'fortress' was carved into the rock and sand of the Libyan Desert. Defences ran in a rough semicircle from the coast thirteen kilometres east of the harbour to the coast fourteen kilometres to the west. The arc was a line of dug-in fortifications almost 50 kilometres in length. By January 1941, Italian engineers and soldiers and Arab labourers had blasted and drilled lines of anti-tank ditches (six metres wide and four metres deep); they had erected concrete machine-gun posts and other reinforcements; laid minefields in abundance and whole gardens of booby traps amidst thickets of barbed wire. The perimeter was punctuated by 'strong points' with the forward ones some 600–800 metres apart and those behind situated to cover the gaps. The strong points were not joined by trenches but they could support each other with gun fire that covered the anti-tank ditch, the wire and the minefields: fire that could sweep the desert for hundreds of metres into no-man's-land. The defenders of Tobruk, whoever they were, would live in this wasteland of rock, dirt and sand, a place where nothing grew but thorny camel bush and the occasional fig tree.

It was an almost featureless landscape that provided little in the way of natural cover for attackers. But for defenders, vulnerable to attack from the air and stretched thin by the sheer length of the perimeter, worn down as much by the weather and the waiting as by the fighting, a siege would be an ordeal of equally testing proportions.

The testing began in December of 1940, just six months after Dunkirk. In the skies above the English Channel the RAF had saved Britain from invasion, but German forces remained unchecked on land, triumphant from Poland to the Pyrenees. 'No force or fortress had withstood the Nazi assault,' wrote the ABC correspondent Chester Wilmot. In the first eighteen months of the war the Allied armies suffered one defeat after another.

But in North Africa Italian forces hesitated. They had crossed the Egyptian border and failed to press on. They dug in along the coast, as if stunned momentarily by news of Mussolini's failed invasion of Greece. In that vulnerable moment the British Western Desert Force under Lieutenant-General Richard O'Connor hit back. Combined with the 6th Australian Division led by Major-General Iven Mackay, the Western Desert Force drove the Italians westward, seizing the garrison towns as they went. Bardia fell on

5 January 1941; after heavy fighting Tobruk was captured on the 22nd, Derna on the 29th, and by early February the remnants of Italian forces were rounded up south of Benghazi. The campaign was a mix of determined Italian resistance and complete routs. The outcome was spectacular. Within a month, O'Connor's forces had swept across more than a thousand kilometres of desert, routed ten Italian divisions, taken 125,000 prisoners and seized hectares of military equipment and supplies.

THE PHOTOGRAPHIC UNIT

War cameramen with the Department of Information's Cinematographic and Photographic Unit filmed the Desert Offensive. The unit was put together in Australia to provide newsreel footage and photographs for propaganda purposes. It was a vital link to the home front, bringing Australians closer to their men in battle than ever before. Imaginations could now be fed not only with newspaper photographs but also with film footage. The newsreel became a routine fixture in cinema programs in the 1930s. It was usually about eight minutes long and lightweight in subject matter – screened for entertainment. But war changed audience expectations. The public wanted more news than they encountered in the papers or heard on the wireless. Newsreel companies were keen to profit from the new demand for a visual war, while the government was anxious to provide effective 'military publicity' in the form of stirring, heartening images from the front.

But the newsreel companies could not raise the capital to send a film unit abroad, so the Commonwealth Government provided the footage. The Department of Information (DOI) funded the filming of war, using distinguished photographer and cameraman Frank Hurley, the much younger Damien Parer, Ron Maslyn Williams, George Silk and the soundman Alan Anderson. To the general public the war newsreels came to them courtesy of familiar names – Movietone and Cinesound – but the DOI's photographic team did the fieldwork. Their film footage and photographs were sent back from the Western Desert and from Tobruk during the siege. They were vetted by the DOI. Frame enlargements from movie footage were passed on to newspapers and magazines and film was passed to the newsreel companies for editing, embellishing with archival footage – composite sequences sometimes combining three or four different actions – and screening. In Sydney in 1941, film goers at the State Theatre who lined up to see Lionel Barrymore in *Dr. Kildare Goes*

Frank Hurley and Alan Anderson recording the light and sound of gunfire during the early morning assault on Tobruk, 21 January 1941.
(Damien Parer. AWM 05655)

Home, or those at the Lyceum to catch Jeanette MacDonald in *Maytime*, were also treated to a newsreel on the Desert Offensive and the capture of Tobruk.

Frank Hurley was in charge of the unit in the field. The new head of DOI, Sir Keith Murdoch, appointed him. The two had first met on the Western Front in 1917. Acquaintance from World War I became an opportunity in the second, and the opportunity presented by the Western Desert Offensive was fit for purpose. The battles were fast moving, the dust horrendous, the light often poor, but stirring images came from the film team in the midst of battle and from the victorious aftermath. Hurley's footage of Italian prisoners, a column of thousands reaching to the horizon, brought cheers from audiences in British cinemas during the grim days of the Blitz. Victory in one part of the world fed morale in another.

One problem was the lapse of time between shooting footage and screening at the movies at home. The Australians who chased Italian forces westward across the top of North Africa were then chased eastward by German forces, with the 9th Division finally besieged in Tobruk. Audiences in 1941 complained about seeing newsreels on victory in the desert while they were reading newspaper articles about the reversals that followed.

During the Allied break-in at Tobruk, in the thick of the fighting, the Photographic Unit's truck ranged alongside the ABC Radio van, with cinematographer Parer in the one and reporter Chester Wilmot in the other. A military policeman is heard shouting: 'Blimey Bert, propaganda goes to war.' This was the beginning of an association that would carry into Tobruk during the siege, and later to Kokoda. Parer's biographer, Neil McDonald, sensed the basis of the friendship:

Wilmot was an intense, heavy-set man, a year older than Parer, who spoke with the slightly British accent required of Australian broadcasters in the 1940s. Often opinionated, frequently in argument (but never personal), he was the kind of tough, competent professional Parer was drawn to … Wilmot came to admire Damien's 'gameness' and his willingness to share the dangers of the soldiers he photographed, just as Parer came to value Wilmot's ability to go beyond simple description and to analyse the political and military strategy underlying the events they were both reporting.

They moved on to Derna where the fighting was again fierce and victory swift. Parer caught the attention of at least one Australian officer who noted his readiness to get near the action to record the experience of the front-line soldier. Another officer was prescient when he judged Parer's bravery would eventually get him killed. Parer was killed on the island of Peleliu in the Pacific in 1944. His legacy includes many fine photographs from the siege of Tobruk and a cinematic contribution to Chester Wilmot's film *Sons of the Anzacs* (1944) – about 60 per cent of the footage in that film came from Parer's Newman-Sinclair 35mm camera.

RETREAT TO THE FORTRESS

The Desert Offensive was a series of well-planned, swift and spectacular victories. Much was made of these successes in England and Australia where there had been so little good news from the battlefronts in Europe. But victory was soon unravelled. O'Connor did not have the resources to press on and secure the western half of Libya (Tripolitania) and British High Command had other priorities. The 6th Division was shipped off to Greece to fight against Hitler's invading forces. The 9th Division – still in training and under equipped – was to garrison the eastern half of Libya (Cyrenaica). The only possible threat to the Allies in this part of the world was a German offensive driving east against the Allies, and this was considered unlikely.

But the unlikely was about to happen. In mid February the German High Command despatched a force to Libya that would soon be known as the *Afrika Korps*. The *Korps* was fresh from victories in Europe, well equipped – especially well armoured – and led by General Erwin Rommel, a Nazi whose legend owed as much to the German propaganda machine as it did to feats on the battlefield. At Benghazi Rommel's forces engaged the British armour and almost destroyed its forward elements, then pressed the British and Australian forces into retreat. Armies were chasing one another back and forth across the top of Africa. One by one the strongholds and garrison towns seized by the Allies in preceding months were given up to Rommel. When Allied forces gathered outside Tobruk, their surviving tank count was thirty. Rommel had three hundred, part of his full complement of five Italian divisions (four infantry and one armoured) and four German battalions (two tank and two machine gun). Without adequate armoured force and support artillery it was impossible for the depleted Allied force to make a stand in the desert. British and Australian troops had either to retreat into the fortress or pull back to the Egyptian border. The choice to be made would have immense implications for the 9th Division, for the war in the desert, for the propaganda war, and ultimately for the fortunes of the Allies.

It was decided. The 9th Division, with support from British gunners and a small complement of Indian soldiers, was to hold Tobruk and thus hold the enemy's advance for at least two months – to buy time for the assembly of reinforcements, armoured troops in particular, for the defence of Egypt. Corporal G. H. Fearnside of the 2/13th Battalion wrote in his diary: 'By the time we got to Tobruk our nerves were ragged. All the way back from Regima we'd steeled ourselves to action which never came and every soldier knows that the waiting before the attack is worst.' There was bitterness among the troops that so much ground won was now lost. There was, in Wilmot's words, 'an itching for retaliation'. As one AIF officer put it, 'We couldn't let it be said that the 9th had lost what the 6th had won.'

Thirty-six hours after the last of the Allied troops withdrew into Tobruk, German forces were probing the outer perimeter. The fortress commander, Lieutenant-General Leslie Morshead, made good use of these hours. Sappers laid mines; the infantry rebuilt barbed-wire entanglements, repaired tank ditches and concrete strong points; signallers plotted vital connections for scarce phone wire; transports carried ammunition, food and water to the forward posts; and gunners dug in their 25 pounders while all over the garrison the 'scroungers' scrounged up what guns and munitions the Italians had failed to destroy. The front line, called the Red Line, was perilously thin in places.

The Allied defending force was just over 35,000 strong. The Australians were mostly infantry from the 9th Division, with a brigade from the 7th, and British soldiers, mostly Royal Horse Artillery men and armoured crewmen. There was also the small complement of 550 men of the 18th Indian Cavalry, under the command of British officers. As figures show, after three months, many British soldiers had been shipped out to other battlefronts, while the Australian complement remained steady until the end of August when the replacement of the Australians began.

Numerical strength of the garrison at Tobruk

	AIF	British
21 April 1941.	14,817	17,742
30 June 1941:	14,326	7,979

The enemy was superior in numbers, armour and fighting experience. They had air superiority too, as the Luftwaffe far outnumbered the RAF in this theatre of war. The defenders had orders from Cairo to hold out for two months, a determination to do so, and a leader who was, almost by instinct, primed to turn defence into attack. That was Morshead.

Morshead was a veteran of the Great War, having served with distinction in Gallipoli and France. Twice wounded, mentioned in dispatches six times and three times decorated for his valour, he was a strict disciplinarian dubbed by his troops 'Ming the Merciless'. But they followed his lead to the letter. At Tobruk he told his commanders: 'There will be no Dunkirk here. If we should have to get out, we shall fight our way out. There is to be no surrender and no retreat.' He said every man, whether cook, clerk or batman, might have to fight. Every man knew that the defence of Egypt depended on holding Tobruk.

On Easter Sunday, 13 April 1941, all the signs indicated a battle was on the way – German staff cars and motorcycles visible at 2000 metres, enemy reconnaissance planes buzzing overhead and dust clouds marking an assemblage of tanks, artillery and lorried infantry beyond the range of the forward guns.

What followed, now registered in history as 'The Easter Battle', set the tone for the entire siege. There were savage preliminaries on Good Friday, Saturday and Easter Sunday, but the decisive moment was still to come. Around midnight the defenders of Post 33 repulsed a force of about thirty Germans in a bout of bloody hand-to-hand fighting. Outnumbered and mortally wounded, Corporal Jack Edmondson fought on with the bayonet. He saved the life of his platoon commander, but he died soon after. He was posthumously awarded the VC – the first won by a member of the 2nd AIF.

Some hours later about 200 German infantry moved through the wire, establishing a bridgehead for their tanks, close to Post 33. Despite heavy fire from British artillery, they held their position. German tanks then massed within the wire, followed by field and anti-tank guns and an infantry battalion. They were coming togther to execute a proven manoeuvre that had smashed defences in Poland, France and Belgium. They expected little in the way of resistance. The tanks pushed forwards some three kilometres inside the perimeter under a steady barrage from the British guns and the guns of the 3rd Australian Anti-Tank Regiment. The air was filled with tracer shells and bullets, 'like a Blackpool illumination,' said one sergeant. The tanks got to within about 600 metres of the British guns when accuracy and the dawning light began to take a toll. The enemy took a pounding. They fell back. They rallied, to try again. But they were isolated. The Australians in the perimeter posts had deliberately held their fire, allowing the enemy tanks to pass and press on; only then did they engage the follow-up forces, the

Shallow trenches cut from rock and sand. Corp. W. Brownrigg and Lance Corp. F. Smith of the 2/23rd Australian Infantry Battalion somewhere in the front line. Tobruk, 1 September 1941. (AWM 020505)

invading anti-tank and field gun units and the infantry. The toll was heavy. German and Italian fighter planes joined the fight but they did not shift the momentum. The Diggers hit the light armour and the infantry with everything they had. The early morning light put the incoming forces at greater disadvantage. German reinforcements were pressed in. Hundreds were shot or captured or driven off. It was a rout.

One of the German tank officers (Lieutenant Schorm, 5th Tank Regiment) would later record the experience in his diary:

Our heavy tanks fire for all they are worth, just as we do, but the enemy, with his superior force and all the tactical advantages of his own territory, makes heavy gaps in our ranks. We are right in the middle of it with no prospect of getting out. From both flanks armour-piercing shells whiz by at 100 metres a second … On the radio – "Right turn!" – "Left turn!" – "Retire!" … Some of our tanks are already on fire. The crews call for doctors who alight to help in this witches' cauldron. English anti-tank units fall upon us with their guns firing in our midst … We bear off to the right … Italian fighter planes come into the fray above us. Two of them crash in our midst. Our optical instruments are spoiled by the dust; nevertheless I register several unmistakable hits. A few anti-tank guns are silenced; some enemy tanks are burning. Just then we are hit and the radio is smashed to bits … our ammunition is giving out. I follow the battalion commander. Our attack is fading out. From every side superior forces of the enemy shoot at us. "Retire". We take a wounded man and two others on board and other tanks do the same …

Somehow Lieutenant Schorm and his near-ruined tank found the gap and escaped the gauntlet of anti-tank guns and perimeter fire, passing a littering of bodies, burning tanks and the wreck of a German Stuka. 'We were lucky to escape alive,' he wrote.

Major J. W. Balfe of the 2/17th Battalion watched the Germans struggling through the wire and later told his story to Chester Wilmot:

There was terrible confusion at the only gap as tanks and infantry pushed their way through it. The crossing was badly churned up and the tanks raised clouds of dust as they went. In addition, there was the smoke of two tanks blazing just outside the wire. Into this cloud of dust and smoke we fired anti-tank weapons, Brens, rifles, and mortars, and the gunners sent hundreds of shells. We shot up a lot of infantry as they tried to get past, and many, who took refuge in the anti-tank ditch, were later captured. It was all I could do to stop the troops following them outside the wire.

TRAPPED

While he took in the shock of defeat, Rommel busied his troops digging in around Tobruk and securing positions on the Egyptian border. Some of his tank commanders had sobbed with shock and shame. The 'Easter Battle' was the first sizeable defeat of German tanks in World War II. The General would restore his forces and try again. Tobruk could not rest. While land forces regrouped, German Stukas pounded the fortress. British anti-aircraft gunners fought off some 677 Stuka attacks in the space of three weeks. The enemy held the sky.

The Easter conflict was not the last major battle on the perimeter, but the pattern of conflict now settled into a stalemate of sorts marked by what Morshead described as 'aggressive patrolling'. The Red Line was, in Chester Wilmot's words, a 'nest of cells – cells of minefields and guns manned by men who were ordered to stand and fight and who did.' From these nests, patrols went out on a mission to monitor, to steal, to kill and thus to never allow the enemy rest or relaxation. It was a ceaseless probing, nipping and slicing at chosen points in enemy lines, mostly at night and rarely in the same place twice. 'I determined we should make no-man's-land *our* land,' wrote Morshead. An Australian newspaper headline had angered the fortress commander. It read 'Tobruk can take it'. 'We're not here to "take it",' he said, 'we're here to give it.' Morshead's attitude was decisive. Despite awful conditions and death ever present, the Australian forces on the perimeter, support troops in the rear and the spirited British gunners all shared an initiative, a moral ascendancy that they never relinquished. The siege was meant to be no more than two months but it went on for eight.

Each unit on the perimeter had a patrol area to cover. The details of any venture into no-man's-land were carefully planned, submitted to brigade HQ for approval and only then put into effect. Diggers on patrol were dressed to a minimum. They travelled light. They carried nothing to reveal their unit and no letters, photographs or mementos that might be used to sway them under interrogation. Gear was modified to eliminate all clanks and rattles and they shared a simple set of hand signals to enable operations in complete silence. There were occasional patrols where such precautions did not apply – these were fast-moving, motorised thrusts supported by tanks, Bren-gun carriers and anti-tank guns hitting the enemy with spectacular impact. The bold and bloody attacks on Carrier Hill on 22 April were a case in point. But regular raids, mounted month after month through the long siege, were generally small scale, silent and mostly at night. Men went out through the wire with blackened faces to creep and crawl close to enemy lines, to plot the positions of minefields, wire and machine-gun posts, note the comings and goings of sentries and spot any vulnerable points in the defences – the prelude to an ambush at some later time.

Near Post 27 on the perimeter, about thirteen kilometres south of Tobruk. Men of the 2/13th Infantry Battalion prepare to go through the wire. (AWM 020784)

At the end of April Rommel tried again, this time an attack from land and air, aimed at seizing the precious vantage point of Hill 209 on the perimeter in the southwestern sector. The 2/24th Battalion held this precinct with the assistance of the British gunners. They were assailed by superior armour and by attack from the air. At some points the line gave way. Strong posts were lost and German fighters seized part of the Hill. After twenty-four hours of savagery and heavy losses on both sides, a reserve battalion from the 2nd perimeter (the Blue Line) was thrown into the fight, now at great disadvantage, for the Germans held the high ground. Between 29 April and 4 May, Allied forces suffered 59 killed and 738 wounded or captured. The German tank officer, Schorm, wrote another entry in his diary on 6 May:

Our opponents are Englishmen and Australians. Not trained attacking troops, but men with nerves and toughness, tireless, taking punishment with obstinacy, wonderful in defence. Ah well, the Greeks also spent ten years before Troy.

Rommel's forces had seized a stretch of the western perimeter and a key vantage point but had not been able to press on. He had not taken Tobruk and his casualties were severe – 167 men killed, 787 wounded or missing and many of his tanks wrecked. As a result he was now out of favour with the German Supreme Command in the Mediterranean. Due to a triumph of message decoding (or 'decryption') known as 'Ultra', Morshead knew that Rommel had been scolded for his brashness, told his casualties were unacceptable, ordered to consolidate and to mount no more attacks on Tobruk. From this point on, the *decrypts* were to weigh mightily on the outcome in the Libyan Desert, culminating in Montgomery's 'prescience' at El Alamein. In May 1941, Ultra intelligence allowed Morshead to prepare in depth without fear of a surprise attack. Morale rose higher still when word came in from Churchill: 'To General Morshead from Prime Minister England. The whole empire is watching your steadfast and spirited defence of this important outpost of Egypt [sic] with gratitude and admiration.'

Rommel dug in on the perimeter, still determined to hold his gains but now endangered by his parlous supply situation. Without Tobruk his supplies – 2000 tons daily – had to come from Tripoli and Benghazi. The Royal Navy and the RAF were harassing Axis shipping on the route from Italy to North Africa, and with the German invasion of Soviet Russia just weeks away, the 'Desert Fox', as Nazi propaganda now labelled him, was not going to be favoured with abundant resources. He was short of everything – food, medicines, water, ammunition, fuel, automotive and tank parts.

In a sense, both sides were trapped in the desert – Morshead by geography, Rommel by logistics – and both shared the ordeals of desert existence – the great Saharan winds known as the 'Khamsin', best defined by Chester Wilmot as 'that fury that periodically scourges the drifting surface of the desert into blinding sandstorm'; both shared the heat, the cold, water that looked like coffee and tasted like sulphur, limited diet, infestations of flies and lice and rats, the threat of dysentery, the danger of boredom, the perils of aggressive patrolling, the constant harassment of shell fire – about 1000 shells a day into the fortress – as well as attack from the sky. Finally, there was that other sharing – the ubiquity of death. Eight hundred and thirty-two Australians died in the siege of Tobruk.

THE UNIT DIVIDED

After the Desert Offensive the Photographic Unit returned to Cairo and there divided. Parer, George Silk and Ron Williams went off to Greece to cover the Allied invasion that was to prove another disaster. Hurley and Anderson went back to Tobruk sensing that the siege was to be a big chapter in the Western Desert story. The other cameras in Tobruk were a few belonging to the AIF's Historical and Film Unit, the one camera permitted to each fighting unit and the unauthorized 'Box Brownies' carried by soldiers. In 1940 the army ordered soldiers to register private cameras with their intelligence officer and to hand them in for operations, but these orders were not generally obeyed. That meant that there were plenty of unauthorized small cameras at Tobruk, but film was unobtainable in the fortress so while unofficial photographs account for

The gunner. Pte. G. Jeffs of the 2/23rd Infantry Battalion beside his Bren Light machine gun somewhere on the Red Line. (AWM 020558)

some memorable images, they are few and far between and many of those since gathered were tiny prints from poor copy negatives, the quality ranging from good to very bad.

The best documented parts of the siege cover the April–May period when Hurley was present – though that documentation has its problems – and the August–September period, when Parer was back and Silk joined him. Another photographer to note was Chester Wilmot, who carried a 'Box Brownie'. His job was words, but his photographs were part of the record he needed to write as he did – with great verve, with an affection for his subject (the Allied fighters) and with an eye for detail and immediacy that is unsurpassed in any other writing about Tobruk.

Hurley called Tobruk in April 'the hottest spot [I] had ever been in' but his footage and his photographs do not quite convey that heat. He took some vivid photographs of the busy harbour, men at their posts and daily routines such as the water cart on its rounds or prisoners at a well, also of harbour wreckage, the clifftop perches of the gunners on the coast and the night bombardments. But he did not endear himself to his soundman, Alan Anderson, or to the troops, with his preference for staging battle action in the full light of day. One soldier told him to go to hell when asked to participate in a re-enactment. Anderson wrote home on this subject. He told his family:

We went right up to the barbed wire at the front line and did some shots there. As usual, we faked a few shots of men with rifles and machine-guns repelling an attack and then afterwards did some shots of a burning tank …We also faked a shot of a plane that had been brought down (Nazi of course) by putting oil and petrol under the motor and lighting it, which gave the impression that the plane had just been brought down in flames.

At other times, however, Hurley captured genuine action. He knew, for example, that he would not have to wait long to get pictures of an attack on the harbour. He and Anderson found an abandoned Italian machine-gun position by the water and readied themselves for a 'shoot', with a ship anchored right in front of them. Hurley fitted his six-inch lens and the two men settled in. Sure enough, as Anderson recalled:

… after a while twelve Stukas arrived [and] began bombing … the ship kept firing until the last Stuka … dropped a bomb down the smokestack and if you look at the film you can see the thing lift out of the water … and start going down.

'The ship kept firing until the last.' Tobruk harbour had to function come what may. The great advantage upon which the Allies depended was access to the sea and supply from Alexandria. The Royal Australian Navy and other ships that 'ran the gauntlet' from Alexandria to Tobruk and back were a key to morale and perseverance inside the fortress. This was called the 'spud run' or 'Tobruk Ferry Service'. The humour belied the perils of the journey. RAN ships carried more than 5000 tons of supplies every month. Supplies in; sick and wounded out. Without these deliveries, the Allied defenders could not have endured the siege. Axis bombers did their best to cut the lifeline. The small flotilla of cargo and RAN vessels that routinely sailed for Tobruk were attacked as soon as they reached 'bomb alley', which was the last 65 kilometres of the journey. Over that final stretch they did not have the protection of British fighters as they came within the Luftwaffe's range. The last leg of the run could be a perilous shoot out, with all deck guns blazing, the 'angry hornet' sound of Stukas coming out of the sky, the hiss of falling bombs, the roar of explosions and the convulsions of the sea all about the ship as it ploughed on towards the harbour and the covering fire of the British gunners set into the rock nests of the escarpment and the gun pits on the clifftops. In April 57 per cent of cargo vessels were forced back to Alexandria. April was the worst month for these attacks but any voyage at any time during the siege was perilous.

One of the earliest convoys out of Tobruk carried the nurses who had tended wounded men during the Western Desert Offensive and the eastward retreat. They were told that Tobruk would more than likely be under heavy artillery fire and was no place for women. They left under protest. The nurses were evacuated on 8 April, just before the siege began.

THE LONG STALEMATE
The configuration of the besieged force was now set. The harbour and town merged into one of three main spheres of the endless labour that was life in the fortress. Morshead required seven infantry battalions to hold the Red Line (the outer perimeter). These forward

troops had their own reserves posted about 800 metres behind the line, reinforced with captured Italian anti-tank guns and machine guns. About three kilometres further inside was the Blue Line, with its own strong posts about 500 metres apart and a patchwork of minefields and barbed-wire thickets to the fore. Behind the Blue Line was a mobile reserve with a motorised battalion at key crossroads, points on an imaginary semicircle that ringed the 'midlands' beyond the town. Between this reserve line and the town the enemy would meet a 'last ditch' reserve – the men who would down tools and move forwards with rifles and bayonets – the cooks, the mechanics, the drivers, the medicos, the bakers, the padres, the water carriers and any other men who could fight. 'There will be no surrender and no retreat.' Morshead made that clear. It was a formidable defence in depth.

Morshead's biggest problem was holding the outer perimeter. Rommel's forces were embedded on Hill 209 and Axis guns could now reach any point in the fortress. Life in Tobruk was life under continual fire. No one in that fortress was free of the dangers or the stress. The Australian infantry took the full force of both. They worked as labourers and fighters. When not fighting they were digging, wiring, laying mines, fetching and carrying out sandbags, metal pickets, ammunition and water. The water ration was three-quarters of a gallon per man per day and less at times. Every drop was manhandled to the perimeter lines. Men in the town might take a sea-water bath. Men on the outer lines rationed every mouthful of drinking water. Battalions were rotated every two weeks to share these privations around. Men moved from the concrete bunkers on the Red Line to the 'rat holes' of the Blue Line, then to the relative comfort of a reserve position and then to the hottest spot – the precinct facing the enemy on Hill 209.

In May and June, Morshead launched a series of attacks in this area, determined to take back the ground lost to the enemy early in May. Some of that lost ground was recovered – the bulge in the line was pressed back – but at great human cost. The garrison could not survive if intense fighting like that continued. Morshead went back to the tactic of aggressive patrolling. The Australians would enforce the faith that no-man's-land belonged to them.

Over several months the raiders' equipment became well adapted. For a time the Australians wore thick socks over their boots. Occasionally they attacked in stockinged feet. Late in the siege they got soft rubber-soled boots to do the job and khaki overalls with elbow and knee patches for crawling over stony ground. The Indians came up with another trick – they made 'silent sandals' out of strips of old motor-tyre. 'Each man carried two or three grenades,' wrote Wilmot,

and a patrol of a dozen normally had one man with a Bren, to be fired from the hip, as many as six with tommy guns, and the remainder with rifles and fixed bayonets. Almost invariably the raiders attacked without artillery support, relying on surprise; but often they withdrew under a protective barrage. Mortars and Bren carriers were usually sent out to positions half a mile or a mile from the enemy post so that they too could give covering fire as the attackers withdrew. The Bren carriers were also used for bringing in wounded.

Patrols were a physical and a mental challenge of the highest order – they called for a combination of careful planning, audacity, fighting skill and courage that played a major part in sustaining self-belief, high morale and the *cocky* self-image that the Diggers so enjoyed. But stresses took a heavy toll. As at Gallipoli, twenty-six years before, sickness became more depleting than wounds. Poor diet – dust-covered stew and chlorine-tasting tea, lack of vitamins and little in the way of fresh fruit – had a wearing effect on the men. The infantry and the ack-ack gunners were near run down. Most infantry battalions had less than three-quarters of their complement available for duties and their equipment, like themselves, was generally stressed. Yet the evidence suggests that morale remained high as did the determination to hold on. German radio propaganda described the besieged forces as 'caught like rats in a trap'. Like raiders going into no-man's-land, the Australians plundered the German simile and turned it to their advantage. They called themselves 'the rats of Tobruk'. 'Trapped', they held out for six months and, in the case of the 2/13th Battalion, for longer.

THE PROPAGANDA WAR

Reporting the siege to people at home was also turned to advantage. The resistance at Tobruk coincided with a low point for the Allies. Although war news was heavily censored, it was impossible to conceal the fact that debacle or near disaster was the mark on many fronts. In the Atlantic the losses were many. The Mediterranean theatre of war was a mess.

Most of North Africa lay in German hands. By mid-year Greece and Crete were lost. In Britain people were living and dying under relentless night bombing raids known as the Blitz. In the months to come Australians would follow the trials of the British people confronting the 'Frankenstein monster' (Robert Menzies' phrase) of fascism. The King and Queen stayed on in London, touring the rubble-strewn streets and the hospitals, and visited the devastated cities in other parts of England. The Australian press celebrated the virtues of British character and race, turning this defiance into a triumph long before it was resolved. If the war was to produce an upsurge of Australian nationalism, it is also true that it inspired a love of England that has rarely been equalled in its intensity.

The siege of Tobruk would play a similarly inspiring part in the propaganda war. Those who scanned the newspaper photos or watched the wartime newsreels in cinemas around Australia were distant witness to Diggers bailing up Italian troops at various places including Tobruk and then to the life of the Australians under siege. Newspaper readers and cinemagoers saw heroic images of the anti-aircraft gunners on the clifftops overlooking Tobruk harbour. They saw the dust-covered infantry men 'living like rats' in the forward trenches, some of them just 400 metres from the enemy. They saw the daily routines – water carriers at work moving across desolate ground to the front lines, naval convoys hastily unloading in Tobruk harbour, night skies lit up by tracers and anti-aircraft fire, patrols preparing to go into no-man's-land, artillery men in clouds of gunsmoke in the sandhills, a cricket match or a sing-song in the rubble-strewn streets of the town, the printing office where soldiers turned out the *Tobruk Truth* and so on. Most of all, what the press photos and newsreel footage from Tobruk were able to convey was the story of an effective resistance – of a siege and a spirit that could not be broken, of a defiance of Nazi power that assured citizens that the war could be won.

At a time when bad news from the battlefronts seemed to be the norm, photographs from Tobruk were priming morale, perhaps reinforcing the apathy at home that so worried the government. The resistance under siege was an epic endeavour, and its place in Australian history was elevated to iconic status by news and newsreel promotion. The name Tobruk became a symbol of the endurance and defiance of Australian troops well before the siege was over.

At the time comparisons with Gallipoli in 1915 were not overlooked, but a better analogy is with 1917 when the Western Front in Europe was a stalemate of mud and blood but Australians at home took comfort from triumphant photographic images of the Light Horse in Palestine and the heroic tale of the Light Horse charge at Beersheba. As if anticipating the need for a 'Tobruk', Charles Chauvel released the feature film *40,000 Horsemen* to rave reviews just months before the siege began. Chauvel's film was a story of how mateship had been forged and tested on the battlefields of World War I and it was intended as a message of inspiration to a new generation of Australian soldiers. The most memorable scenes were found in the re-enacted cavalry charge at Beersheba, shot in the sandhills of Cronulla and on level ground near Orange in country New South Wales. The siege of Tobruk began not long after the film's successful tour of Australian cinemas.

The visual record from Tobruk is an impressive one although it does not have the same drama, the same visceral edge, as the Western Front record where a living landscape of farms, fields and forests, of towns and cities too, was devastated beyond recognition, leaving no more than an eerie, smoke-ridden, skeletal residue to confront the viewer. There is no recorded drama in the flatness and emptiness of the Libyan Desert to match. Nor did the besieged at Tobruk suffer bouts of mass annihilation to compare with Pozières or Ypres. The blank stares of exhausted men shelled to the brink of catatonia are not a common part of the Tobruk record.

In both wars the record of death was censored but it seems the ruling of 'no photographs of allied dead' was strictly

Where will the next shell land? Pte. J. Collins sits out an artillery bombardment in a front-line post sometime in August 1941.
(George Silk. AWM 009513)

followed at Tobruk in 1941. Very little of human loss and suffering survives on the visual record. The stresses are not evident in the photographic stills as they are in the record from the Western Front where it seems to be almost inescapable. The strains of exhaustion and long-term entrapment, for instance, produced many psychological casualties at Tobruk and consequences such as self-inflicted wounds, but unlike 1917 there is no photography that conveys this suffering. And yet the visual record of the war in the Western Desert is still tremendously informative and valuable. There are many fine photo portraits of individual soldiers. Some of Parer's action shots (on land and at sea) manage to catch the intensity and strain of the moment. The techniques of night photography, much improved in the inter-war period, are put to work at Tobruk to fine effect. And the propaganda angle that was, after all, the photographers' commission, has produced some remarkable images to capture the aggressive, cheery spirit that Morshead insisted upon.

The official photography is mostly news and newsreel photography shot consciously for home-front consumption. Some of the posed shots of gunners at the ready, the camera angled upward, could readily double as studies for heroic sculpture. At the same time, some of the soldier photographers' informal photos well complement the dutiful or artistic shots of the official photographers. Private R. K. Bryant's photo memories, for example, provide a record of a small fighting unit, the camaraderie, daily routines and the business of war – the care of their Breda gun, the unit in action, the loss of a comrade, the men left behind. This is a 'close-up', a visual sequence of shared experience over many months at war, and it is a record of the special bond forged between men in the front line.

THE RELIEF OF TOBRUK

At Headquarters in Cairo, General Sir Thomas Blamey pressed hard for the relief of the Tobruk forces. He wanted the Australian divisions fighting together, as did the government in Canberra. In July 1941 Blamey used the poor health of the 9th Division men to force the issue. When British command finally agreed, the planners turned their attention to the practical problems of how to ship more than 15,000 British and Polish troops into Tobruk and a similar number of Australians out, through a port that had no surviving jetties and, in all probability, remained a port under air attack.

The changeover began in August and went on through speedy night runs in September and October. Some of this was filmed by Damien Parer who made two more forays to the fortress by sea. Against all odds, the relief of Tobruk went without a hitch until the final drop-off and pick-up operation on the night of 25 October. The 2/13th Battalion was last to leave. The battalion was waiting in the storage tunnels by the harbour when news of disaster came through. Enemy bombers had raided the convoy, sunk the cruiser HMS *Latona* and damaged the British destroyer *Hero*. After picking up survivors, *Hero* turned back to Alexandria. The 2/13th would have to stay on. The battalion fought on at Tobruk until 16 December. It was the only Australian battalion to leave by road.

The holding of Tobruk made a sizeable dent in the aura of invincibility associated with Rommel's campaigns. In the Easter Battle a German machine-gun battalion was ruined and a Panzer regiment routed. Thereafter the siege was a long stalemate, punctuated by several full-scale battles and hundreds of deadly skirmishes, by continual shelling and attacks from the air. The siege divided Rommel's forces and halted his advance on Egypt. Axis forces were stalled in the Libyan Desert from April to December and while the fortress held there was no solution to Rommel's desperate supply situation. The 9th Division, the British artillerymen and the Indian cavalrymen held out against Axis forces for six months, and the 2/13th Battalion was there, with British and Polish replacements, for two months more. Rommel said he would drive them into the sea. They pinned him down in the Libyan Desert. They escaped to Egypt, to recuperate and get ready for more of the same and then they went back to the desert, to a little-known place east of Tobruk called El Alamein.

For Australia, the human toll at Tobruk was a heavy one – 3009 casualties including 832 men killed and 941 men taken prisoner.

WESTERN DESERT OFFENSIVE

The Western Desert Offensive against the Italian fortresses on the Libyan coast was a series of swift and spectacular victories. In little more than two months (December 1940 and January 1941) British and Australian forces overwhelmed the garrisons at Sidi Barrani, Salum, Bardia, Tobruk and Benghazi. They took 130,000 prisoners, captured almost 400 tanks and about 8000 guns.

The Department of Information's Photographic Unit was nearly in the right place at almost the right time. Frank Hurley, Ron Maslyn Williams, George Silk, the soundman Alan Anderson and their driver, Pambo Morrison, chased the fast-moving battlefront across the desert.

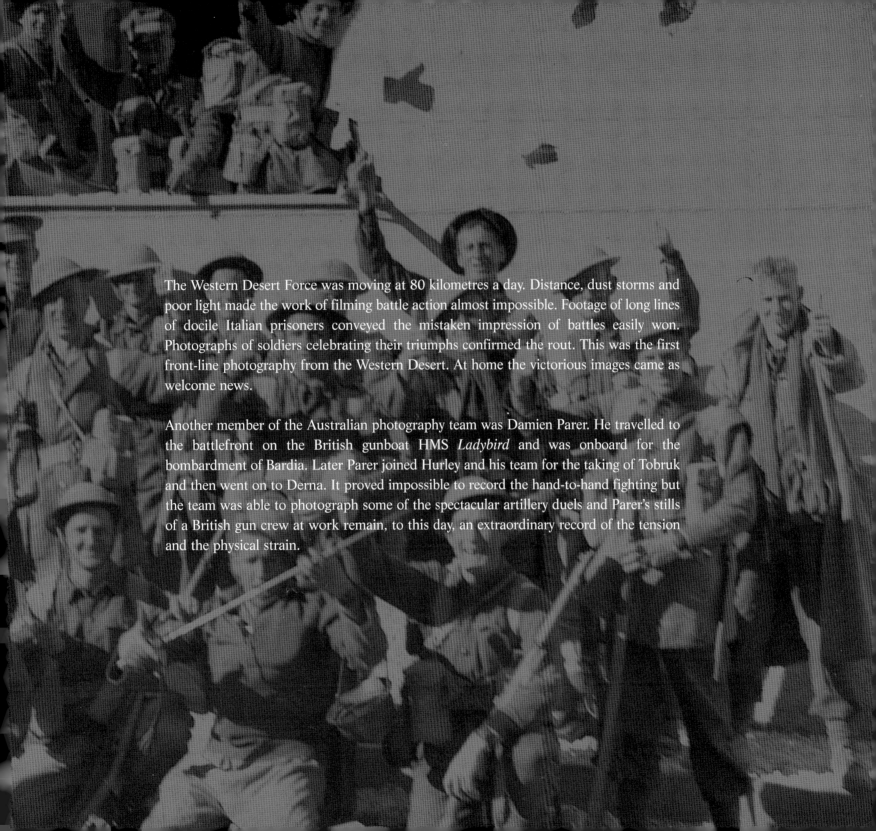

The Western Desert Force was moving at 80 kilometres a day. Distance, dust storms and poor light made the work of filming battle action almost impossible. Footage of long lines of docile Italian prisoners conveyed the mistaken impression of battles easily won. Photographs of soldiers celebrating their triumphs confirmed the rout. This was the first front-line photography from the Western Desert. At home the victorious images came as welcome news.

Another member of the Australian photography team was Damien Parer. He travelled to the battlefront on the British gunboat HMS *Ladybird* and was onboard for the bombardment of Bardia. Later Parer joined Hurley and his team for the taking of Tobruk and then went on to Derna. It proved impossible to record the hand-to-hand fighting but the team was able to photograph some of the spectacular artillery duels and Parer's stills of a British gun crew at work remain, to this day, an extraordinary record of the tension and the physical strain.

C Company men of the 2/11th Battalion, on the escarpment south of Tobruk Harbour, 22 January 1941. They had over-whelmed ack-ack gun positions and paused for a photo before moving on to the town. (Frank Hurley. AWM 005392)

After the bombardment. Australians inside Tobruk, 23 January 1941. (Frank Hurley. AWM 005607)

The official photographers were under orders to ignore the carnage of the Western Desert Offensive. This shot of an Italian gunner, dead beside his gun, is a rare one. (Frank Hurley. AWM 005599)

Everyone is happy, expectant, eager. Old timers say the spirit is the same as in the last war. Each truck-load was singing as we drove to the assembly point in the moonlight. All ranks carried a rum issue against the bleak morning. At 1930 hours we passed the 'I' tanks, against the skyline like a fleet of battle cruisers, pennants flying ... Infantry moving up all night.

Diarist of the 16th Brigade, 6th Division AIF, 2 January 1941

One of a series of stills taken by Damien Parer, revealing the strain and tension of the artillery duels. Here British gunners are at work during the bombardment of Derna, 31 January 1941. (Damien Parer. AWM 005652)

LEFT: The victors. Men of the 2/2nd Battalion celebrate the taking of Bardia with a feast of captured food, wine, cigars and goat. This was part of a series of photos taken by Frank Hurley on the theme of triumph in the Western Desert. (Frank Hurley. AWM 004906)

Parer was among them, busy with his camera, sometimes standing erect, sometimes crouched on one knee.

John Hetherington, *Nine Profiles*

British tanks and trucks roll on to Derna, 30 January 1941. (Damien Parer. AWM 005656)

An oil tanker burning in Tobruk Harbour provided Prime Minister Robert Menzies with a 'hot shot'. Menzies was an avid amateur cameraman. Some of the 16mm colour footage that he shot in the Middle East, en route to London in February 1941, is now preserved at the National Film and Sound Archive/Screensound.
(Damien Parer. AWM 005853)

RIGHT: Troops from the 1st Anti-Tank Company listening to an address by Prime Minister Robert Menzies: 'It is not that you have come here to capture this desolate land but you have played a glorious part in helping to smash the Italian Empire,' he told them.
(Damien Parer. AWM 005858)

It was some days before all the enemy dead had been found and buried. Long columns of dejected prisoners in drab olive-green and khaki streamed eastwards. In the whole battle, 38,300 prisoners, 237 guns and 73 tanks were captured.

Gavin Long, *To Benghazi*

Some of the Italians carried pocketsful of grenades. It was necessary to search prisoners for these and other weapons as soon as possible. Tobruk, 23 January 1941. (Frank Hurley. AWM 005405)

RIGHT: Some of the footage in wartime newsreels showed columns of Italian prisoners stretching to the horizon. These prisoners are coming into Sidi Barrani on 14 December 1940. Audiences in Australian cities, and in London, cheered at these sequences, and stills from this footage have become part of Digger legend. (Frank Hurley. AWM 004399)

Very few photos of the retreat that followed the Western Desert Offensive have survived. Gnr. R. K. Bryant of 8 Battery, 2/3rd Light Anti-Aircraft Regiment, took a few of the rare surviving images. The photograph shows Bryant and his comrades camped on the side of the Derna-to-Tobruk road during the retreat, early in April 1941.
From left to right: Gnr. J. Buntz, Gnr. J. W. Croft, Gnr. Taylor and Gnr. R. K. Bryant.
(Lent by R. K. Bryant. AWM P01260.006)

Has been a month of disappointment, from a marvellous time at Derna to something rotten and fearful never knowing when one will come over with your S.X. [number] on it.

Private Tom Derrick, 2/48th Battalion, 30 April 1941

THE RED LINE

Today has been distressingly hot — about 115 I should think. Consider your plight for a moment — living in shallow holes in rocky ground, not a tree with[in] hundreds of miles, no shade except what we make with bits of wood and so on, none of the luxuries of life such as eats and drinks, and nowhere to go and no respite.

Lieutenant Tas Gill, 2/48th Battalion, 1 June 1941

Allied forces withdrew into Tobruk on 8 April. Their orders were to hold the fortress for two months, to conduct a defence that was as mobile as possible and take every opportunity to hinder the enemy's concentration by offensive action. Their commander Lieutenant-General Morshead was a battalion commander on the Western Front in World War I. His experience stood him in good stead for the kind of semi-static warfare that would follow.

Morshead conceived a defence based on a strong perimeter called the Red Line, supported by secondary and tertiary lines, with instructions to hold at all costs. From the outer perimeter the Australians mounted their patrols into no-man's-land and their raids into enemy lines, mostly by night. It was a technique developed in the last year of the war on the Western Front, keeping the enemy off-balance and unable to counter in kind.

Throughout April and into May, German forces attempted a number of combined infantry-armour assaults, but they lost many tanks at the hands of the British and Australian artillerymen and their retreats left infantrymen exposed to assaults by the Australian fighters, resulting in large numbers of the enemy being captured or killed. The photographer Frank Hurley said April in Tobruk was the hottest spot he had ever been in, but his photographic record does not convey the heat of that warfare. So much of the action took place, for tactical reasons, in the poor light of the early morning or the dark of night. Damien Parer would later say that in desert warfare everything is just a little beyond your grasp. It was possible to film the Stukas coming in, or anti-aircraft action around the harbour, but on the outer perimeter where so much happened under the cover of dust storms or poor light, and where the Australians were secreted in foxholes trying to ambush the enemy, the chances for a photographer, let alone a film cameraman with tripod, were few and far between. The result is a photographic record that does not include the Easter Battle but does capture something of the fortifications on the perimeter, the life for the Australians in the front line and the preliminaries to their aggressive patrolling.

Some parts of the Red Line or the outer perimeter at Tobruk were just 400 metres from the enemy. Forward posts such as this one (location not identified) were completely isolated during the daylight hours. (George Silk. AWM 009514)

LEFT: A Bren gunner in action somewhere on the front line. (George Silk. AWM 009510)

We shot up a lot of infantry as they tried to get past, and many, who took refuge in the anti-tank ditch, were later captured.

Major J. W. Balfe, 2/17th Battalion

D Company men, 2/13th Battalion, on the front line, 30 April 1941. They were positioned a couple of hundred metres from the wire. (Frank Hurley. AWM 007480)

A patrol from the 2/13th Battalion making its way through a gap in the barbed-wire entanglements, 8 September 1941. Most patrols were at night. Photographs such as this were probably taken in a quiet sector and the patrol enacted for the camera. (AWM 020780)

AUSSIES

AFTER CRETE DISASTER ANZAC TROOPS ARE NOW BEING RUTHLESSLY SACRIFICED BY ENGLAND IN TOBRUCH AND SYRIA.
TURKEY HAS CONCLUDED PACT OF FRIENDSHIP WITH GERMANY. ENGLAND WILL SHORTLY BE DRIVEN OUT OF THE MEDITERRANEAN. OFFENSIVE FROM EGYPT TO RELIEVE YOU TOTALLY SMASHED.

YOU CANNOT ESCAPE.

OUR DIVE BOMBERS ARE WAITING TO SINK YOUR TRANSPORTS. THINK OF YOUR FUTURE AND YOUR PEOPLE AT HOME.

COME FORWARD - SHOW WHITE FLAGS AND YOU WILL BE OUT OF DANGER !

SURRENDER !!

'You cannot escape.' The punchline in a leaflet dropped over the front lines at Tobruk. Another propaganda leaflet called on the defenders to surrender and concluded: 'Single soldiers waving white handkerchiefs will not be fired on.' One of Gen. Morshead's reports joked that due to the shortage of water there were no clean handkies available. (George Silk. AWM 009509)

LEFT: A soldier's snap of life on the front line, July 1941. G. G. Anderson and Capt. Ian Malloch MC of the 2/24th Battalion. (AWM P00237.036)

Received ammunition. No idea how 15 Platoon and Company Headquarters are faring. 13 Platoon lost forward section Post S1. Enemy have occupied this post in strength. Also have light gun on ridge above this post making holding of this platoon area untenable.

Captain J. S. Rosel, 2/24th Battalion

The sandbags were being cut by fire and the sand draining on to the Bren [gun] prevented it from firing more than single shots. I was using a German machine pistol which stopped for the same reason. I then used my rifle. As they were coming from behind the tank in two's and three's single shots were enough.

Signaller L. L. White, 2/28th Battalion, 3 August 1941

Post Z101, the last post on the eastern perimeter. Men of the 9th Division Army Service Corps are looking towards enemy positions. They are armed with an Italian Breda gun and rifles. Cpl. Butcher and Drivers George Lawson, Skews, Shoobridge and M. J. Chalmers made up this *scratch* unit. (AWM 020699)

LEFT: Bringing in the wounded through a gap in the wire entanglements, 17 September 1941. (AWM 020669)

Post R8 on the perimeter, about fourteen kilometres south west of Tobruk Harbour. It is 28 May. A truce has been called to allow German soldiers to recover their dead and wounded after a night attack and the loss of Post R7. As the truce came to an end these men of the 2/13th Battalion were once again out of sight. (AWM 128992)

Rats of Tobruk. Headquarters of the 2/23rd
Infantry Battalion, 30 August 1941.
(AWM 020483)

Early in July there was a disturbing
increase in enemy shelling on the forward
defence areas. More than 2,500 shells
per day, about 1,500 in the western
sector alone, rained down for a period
of two days ending on 4 July.

Barton Maughan, *Tobruk and El Alamein*

Tobruk cemetery. A soldier's photograph of Pte. J. Smith, 2/17th Batallion, at the grave of Cpl. Jack Edmondson. Edmondson was awarded the Victoria Cross posthumously, for action on 13 April 1941. This was the first VC to go to a 2nd AIF soldier.
(AWM P00426.005)

During the siege of Tobruk, a newsreel screened in Australian cinemas on the presentation of the late Cpl. Jack Edmondson's VC to his parents. This private photograph captures a moment in the presentation ceremony – Mr. and Mrs. J. W. Edmondson at Admiralty House, Sydney, 27 September 1941. (AWM P01170.001)

THE GUNNERS

*The first shell fell short. 'Cock em up a bit boys,'
said the Colonel. We did, and the second shell fell
dead between the two leading vehicles. We kept on
firing and they disappeared in a cloud of dust –
and stayed out of range for the rest of the day.*

Sergeant E. D. Rule, 2/28th Battalion

'British artillery was the rock on which the two main German assaults in April and May finally broke,' wrote the ABC reporter Chester Wilmot. In the months of stalemate that followed, the British gunners of the Royal Horse Artillery (RHA) continued to be a vital part of the defence, along with the Australian 2/12th Field Regiment and the 'Bush artillery', the infantry units that turned themselves into gunners using captured Italian guns. With the exception of the Hill 209 area, often called 'The Salient', Australian infantry patrols held the enemy well back from the outer perimeter or Red Line while the British and Bush artillery subdued the German guns as best they could. Life in the fortress would have been far more perilous without an artillery that regularly searched out German gun positions.

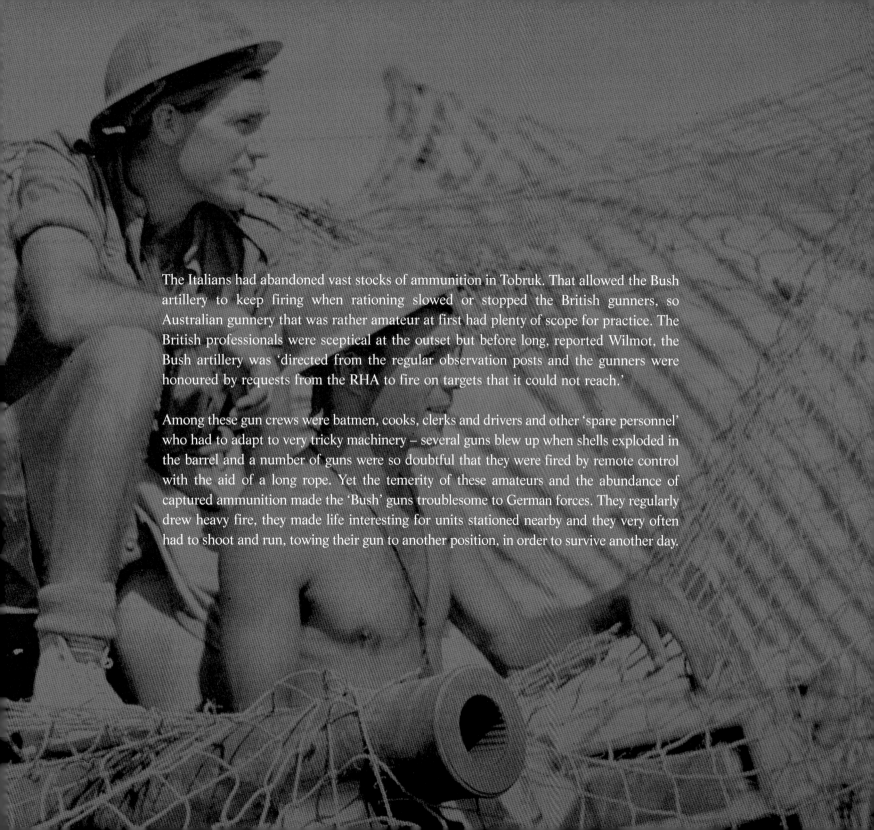

The Italians had abandoned vast stocks of ammunition in Tobruk. That allowed the Bush artillery to keep firing when rationing slowed or stopped the British gunners, so Australian gunnery that was rather amateur at first had plenty of scope for practice. The British professionals were sceptical at the outset but before long, reported Wilmot, the Bush artillery was 'directed from the regular observation posts and the gunners were honoured by requests from the RHA to fire on targets that it could not reach.'

Among these gun crews were batmen, cooks, clerks and drivers and other 'spare personnel' who had to adapt to very tricky machinery – several guns blew up when shells exploded in the barrel and a number of guns were so doubtful that they were fired by remote control with the aid of a long rope. Yet the temerity of these amateurs and the abundance of captured ammunition made the 'Bush' guns troublesome to German forces. They regularly drew heavy fire, they made life interesting for units stationed nearby and they very often had to shoot and run, towing their gun to another position, in order to survive another day.

Our gun drill wasn't very good and our fire orders would have shocked the R.H.A. [Royal Horse Artillery] but we got shells away.

Sergeant E. D. Rule, 2/28th Battalion

Manhandling a captured 149mm Italian field gun. Here men of the 2/28th Battalion combine with soldiers from the 104th Royal Horse Artillery, 18 September 1941. (AWM 020648)

The 60 pounders were somewhat short of ammunition but fortunately some more rounds have arrived. Artillery here is working under difficulties and we are in need of a flash-spotting and sound-ranging group to fix hostile batteries and an occasional sortie.

Diarist, 2/12th Field Regiment

Gunners duck for cover as their field gun fires. Some of the captured guns were so dangerous they had to be fired at a distance, behind a barricade, using an improvised lanyard. Faulty ammunition and premature explosions were the main problem. (AWM 020651)

RIGHT: Beneath camouflage nets, heavy clouds of dust and smoke engulf a 25-pound gun of the 107th Regiment, Royal Horse Artillery, 27 August 1941. (AWM 020377)

Infantry units made use of captured Italian field guns. Few of the guns had sights or instruments. The scratch crews, converted infantrymen, got direction by squinting down the barrel and range by trial and error. They became known as the 'Bush artillery'. In this photo members of the 2/17th Infantry Battalion are in action with a captured Italian 75mm field gun, 27 August 1941. (AWM 020282)

From an infantryman's plaything the Bush Artillery became an important part of Tobruk's artillery defences.

Chester Wilmot, ABC War Correspondent

Each troop in the salient must now fire its 100 rounds per gun per day.

Col. S. T. Goodwin, 2/12th Field Regiment

Another carefully composed portrait. Men of the 'Bush artillery', 2/17th Battalion, search the horizon for signs of the enemy, Tobruk, 27 August 1941. (AWM 020277)

RIGHT: Some photo portraits taken at Tobruk expressed the progress of photography as an art form in the period between the two world wars. The low-angled shot, carefully composed to convey virility and heroic force, was now established in film and stills photography. Here the subject is a gun crew from 2/17th Battalion, 27 August 1941. (AWM 020286)

Night work. A 3.7
anti-aircraft gun
firing at enemy
aircraft, Tobruk,
15 September 1941.
(AWM 020738)

Tobruk, 10 October
1941. Anti-aircraft
batteries in action
during a night raid.
(AWM 021076)

ABOVE LEFT: A gun crew in action against enemy aircraft, 6 September 1941. These are men of the 3rd Anti-Aircraft Regiment using an Italian Breda gun mounted on a Chevrolet two-ton truck. (AWM 020582)

ABOVE: Innovation. A rear gunner's canopy and machine gun from a JU87 (a Stuka dive bomber) shot down over Tobruk. The gun was put to work in a bunker as part of Tobruk's anti-aircraft defences. June 1941. (AWM 007973)

LEFT: Anti-aircraft gunners in action, Tobruk, 1941. (AWM 040609)

THE BATTLE FOR THE HARBOUR

Unloading parties swarm aboard and slide ammunition down wooden chutes into one barge, while the rest of the cargo is dumped anyhow into the other. As soon as the troops are off, the crew start bringing wounded aboard in stretchers.

Chester Wilmot

The harbour was the defenders' lifeline. Unable to take Tobruk by land, Rommel hoped to close the harbour by attack from the air. If it could not be closed then it might be possible to so restrict the arrival and unloading of supplies as to starve the defence into submission. Between 10 April and 9 October more than 3000 German and Italian aircraft attacked the harbour in the course of some 750 raids. A conservative estimate puts the cost at 150 planes shot down and twice that number damaged. The harbour was never closed and the defence became more effective as time went on, as the ack-ack gunners grew in number and their skills sharpened.

By June small ships and lighters or barges were able to unload in daylight. But the best of the German pilots could wreak terrible havoc. One of them, whom the defenders nicknamed 'Jimmy', would glide in from a certain direction while other Stukas roared in from another to draw the fire. On one occasion Jimmy caught a group of soldiers lining up for cigarettes. His bombs killed eleven and wounded many more.

Although the Stukas were subdued, unloading ships in daylight remained a very dangerous business. To reduce the dangers, incoming vessels would lay up alongside one of the wrecks in the harbour, shielded by huge camouflage nets. Two of the wrecks were Italian ships. Another was HMS *Ladybird*, the small destroyer that participated in the bombardment of Bardia and then joined the 'spud run' – the supply ships from Alexandria and Mersa Matruh that sustained Tobruk.

HMS *LadyBird* joined the defence of the harbour early in May during some of the fiercest of the Stuka 'parades,' as the defenders called them. On 12 May the ship took a direct hit in the stern during an air attack. Another bomb crashed through the deck, blew up the boiler room and started a fuel fire that spread fast. Sailors on the for'ard guns kept firing while some were evacuated, others leapt into oil flames on the water and the ship slowly went down in the shallows, leaving the for'ard guns intact. HMS *Ladybird* was a wreck but its guns were now a part of the harbour's fixed defences.

Fred and Mick, Service Corps men on combat duties. Fred Frazer of Gulargambone (NSW) and Mick Monta of Melbourne (standing) on lookout near Tobruk harbour, 25 September 1941. They were with the Army Service Corps, 9th Division. (AWM 020621)

The Fritz Air Force seems to have things their own way, fear the worst and cannot hold much chance for our return home.

Private Tom Derrick, 2/48th Battalion, 29 April 1941

A Scottish anti-aircraft gun crew in action on Tobruk Harbour using a Bofors 40mm anti-aircraft gun, 15 September 1941. (AWM 020737)

A spotter on watch from the gun pit. Alec Reid of Glasgow, searching for German dive bombers. (AWM 020751)

Harbourside gun crew on the lookout, 17 September 1941. (AWM 020673)

RIGHT: A Bren gunner in action amidst the rubble of the town. (AWM 009829)

*In June there were 134 bombing raids on the
fortress, in addition to 39 reconnaissance flights.*

Barton Maughan, *Tobruk and El Alamein*

The armed boarding vessel *Chakla* under bomber attack in Tobruk Harbour, 29 April 1941. *Chakla* was sunk during this attack. The photograph is a still taken from a Cine newsreel, the footage shot by Damien Parer. (Damien Parer AWM 127950)

The effect of a thousand-pound bomb on a small ship at the wharf in Tobruk Harbour, 7 May 1941. (Frank Hurley. AWM 007578)

Great innings Ladybird and we are all extremely sorry that it has ended. We will beat them on any wicket.

Lieutenant-General Morshead to Lieutenant-Commander J. F. Blackburn, 12 May 1941

The covering guns. When HMS *Ladybird* was sunk in Tobruk Harbour on 12 May several of her guns remained above the water line and so were put to good use thereafter. The embedded *Ladybird* became a fixed battery. Here a couple of Royal Artillery men from the 14th Light Anti-Aircraft Regiment are carrying out maintenance work on one of *Ladybird's* guns, 5 September 1941. (AWM 020575)

April 1941. The never-ending task of unloading supplies and munitions. Work such as this was always hurried, the aim being never to be caught by the German dive bombers, to get supplies secreted away, and to get the ships out of harbour as quickly as possible.

(Frank Hurley. AWM 007501)

We hadn't tasted any [fresh meat] for three months. And was it appreciated? We smacked our lips after each mouthful and said My, this is delicious. This did much to buck up our spirits.

War Diary, 2/48th Battalion, July 1941

HMS *Ladybird* also made a handsome diving platform for the artillerymen in quiet times.
(AWM 020579)

April 1941. The official photographers routinely laid up around the harbour waiting for an attack to film or photograph. While they waited they took shots of the endless activity related to the supply of the garrison. Here stores and ammunition are unloaded onto lighters.
(Frank Hurley. AWM 007507)

BATHING IN A SHAVING MUG

We get one bottle of water per day, besides a spot of tea, and of course it's impossible to keep water cool – it's always warm and tastes very brackish. The longing for something cool, or cold, is maddening... Thank God for the day when we are blasted, driven or fight our way out of this place.

Lieutenant Tas Gill, 2/48th Battalion, 1 June 1941

When Rommel failed to seize the town and harbour in the April and May battles, he directed his bombers against Tobruk's water supply. Drinkable water was a prized possession. He hoped to 'thirst' the defenders into submission, but anti-aircraft gunners fiercely defended the water resources within the fortress and they survived the siege.

When the Italians fled the fortress early in April, they sabotaged many guns and destroyed a great deal of ammunition but they left the water supply intact, perhaps assuming that as prisoners they might need some of it. They also left an excellent cache of bottled mineral water called *Recoaro*. It was said that *Recoaro* was the only water that Italian officers drank in the Libyan garrisons. The invaders found a huge iron shed packed with cases of it,

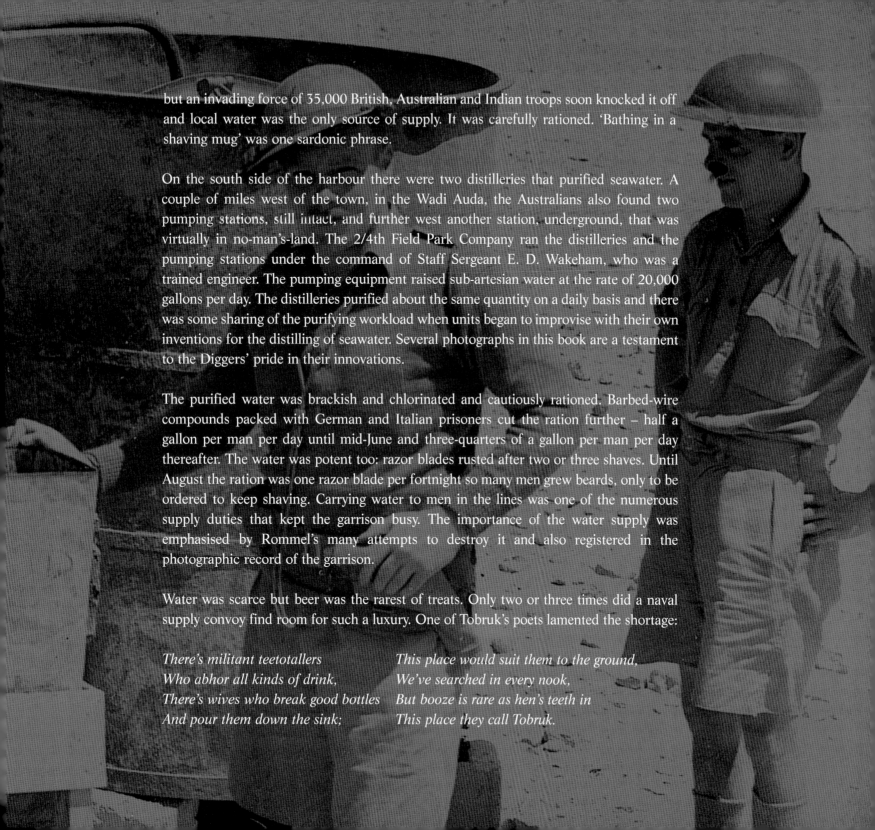

but an invading force of 35,000 British, Australian and Indian troops soon knocked it off and local water was the only source of supply. It was carefully rationed. 'Bathing in a shaving mug' was one sardonic phrase.

On the south side of the harbour there were two distilleries that purified seawater. A couple of miles west of the town, in the Wadi Auda, the Australians also found two pumping stations, still intact, and further west another station, underground, that was virtually in no-man's-land. The 2/4th Field Park Company ran the distilleries and the pumping stations under the command of Staff Sergeant E. D. Wakeham, who was a trained engineer. The pumping equipment raised sub-artesian water at the rate of 20,000 gallons per day. The distilleries purified about the same quantity on a daily basis and there was some sharing of the purifying workload when units began to improvise with their own inventions for the distilling of seawater. Several photographs in this book are a testament to the Diggers' pride in their innovations.

The purified water was brackish and chlorinated and cautiously rationed. Barbed-wire compounds packed with German and Italian prisoners cut the ration further – half a gallon per man per day until mid-June and three-quarters of a gallon per man per day thereafter. The water was potent too: razor blades rusted after two or three shaves. Until August the ration was one razor blade per fortnight so many men grew beards, only to be ordered to keep shaving. Carrying water to men in the lines was one of the numerous supply duties that kept the garrison busy. The importance of the water supply was emphasised by Rommel's many attempts to destroy it and also registered in the photographic record of the garrison.

Water was scarce but beer was the rarest of treats. Only two or three times did a naval supply convoy find room for such a luxury. One of Tobruk's poets lamented the shortage:

There's militant teetotallers   *This place would suit them to the ground,*
Who abhor all kinds of drink,   *We've searched in every nook,*
There's wives who break good bottles   *But booze is rare as hen's teeth in*
And pour them down the sink;   *This place they call Tobruk.*

At first the water tasted like medecine, but after a while it seemed quite good unless you happened to have some sweet water with which to compare it. One night a new arrival brought some water from Alexandria. In the mess a precious jugful was passed around. We drank it neat.

Chester Wilmot

The rationing of water brought about some novel economies in the washing process. Cpl. Vernon Jack from East Malvern in Victoria washed his socks in a biscuit tin, 25 September 1941. His bandaged pipe seems to be another make-do measure. (AWM 020613)

LEFT: Men of the 9th Division Cooking Corps carrying water and provisions to troops in the forward area. The cookhouse, at this point, was near the top of the rise. (AWM 020615)

Australian troops drawing their ration of water from a truck operated by a British Royal Army Service Corps Unit. The truck is of captured Italian origin – 'Acqua Potabile' (drinkable water).

(AWM 040634)

The men are in good fettle and as eager as ever. They are a grand lot. Health is good considering the conditions — a dust storm practically every other day and 1/2 a gallon of water a day.

Lieutenant-General Leslie Morshead

The bathroom, Australians at work. Tobruk, October 1941. (AWM 020893)

ABOVE LEFT: More innovation. A patent still for purifying water photographed by Frank Hurley on 7 May 1941. The still was invented by Lt. J. Blair-Yuill, 345 Coy Royal Army Service Corps (centre of picture). Many units in Tobruk improvised stills similar to this one for the distilling of seawater. (Frank Hurley. AWM 007527)

Soldiers drawing water from a natural well, Tobruk, 8 September 1941. (AWM 020777)

The Italians had left substantial stores of Chianti, cognac, aniseed brandy and a mineral water named Recoaro. The Chianti was good but the brandy was fiery and the aniseed worse. The Recoaro was excellent.

Chester Wilmot, *Desert Siege*

'Bloody hard to get.' The supply convoys from Alexandria rarely had space to bring beer to the besieged men of Tobruk. The shortage theme figured in a wall painting by Sapper 'Doc' Dawes, an Engineer with the 2/23rd Australian Field Company.
(AWM 020096)

Tobruk, 25 April 1941. The water cart brings Italian prisoners their daily ration. (Alan Anderson. AWM 007584)

Italian prisoners filling their water bottles in one of the prison compounds at Tobruk, 28 April 1941. (Frank Hurley. AWM 007567)

Bath day. Men in the town could bathe in the sea but otherwise a wash called for careful, sparing use of the water. (AWM 040632)

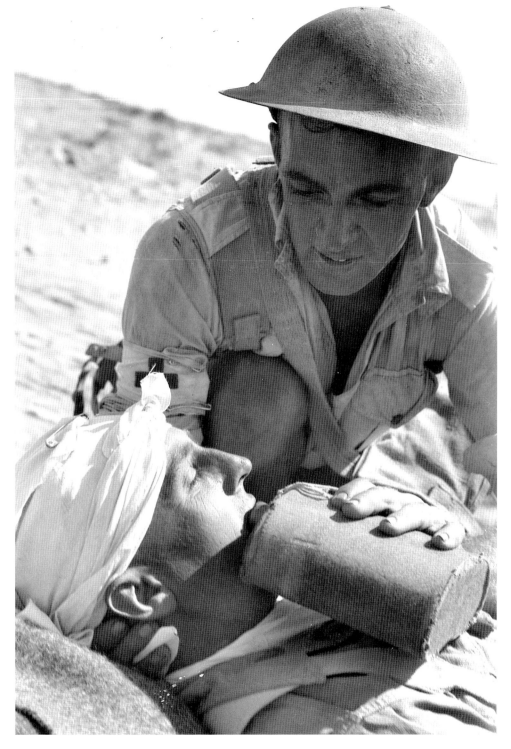

The high standard of health which had prevailed since leaving Palestine declined on entering Tobruk, chiefly because of the increasing heat, the difficulty of obtaining adequate quantities of water for washing purposes, and the innumerable flies. Gastroenteritis became very prevalent.

Medical officer's report, War Diary,
2/13th Battalion, June 1941

A stretcher-bearer with water for the wounded, 15 September 1941. (AWM 020747)

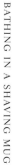

ROUTINES

The rations were good and well balanced but for long, unbroken periods, were 'hard' and monotonous and in the forward posts had to be eaten 'hard', except at night, when a hot meal ... was brought forward. Many men tended to go off their food.

Barton Maugham, *Tobruk and El Alamein*

As at Gallipoli, there was no escape from the dangers or the stresses; in both places men were killed by enemy fire while swimming in the sea. When not fighting, men on duty were digging, wiring, laying mines, fetching and carrying rolls of wire, sandbags, metal pickets, ammunition and water. Battalions were rotated every two or three weeks. Soldiers moved from the concrete bunkers or sandbagged posts on the Red Line to the 'rat holes' of the secondary line, then to the relative comfort of a reserve position.

Living in the town had its advantages but men still found themselves 'dossing' in tunnels cut out of the escarpment or in a 'lean-to' composed from the rubble of houses. Some of them reinforced the rooms of surviving abodes making them strong enough to withstand all but a direct hit. Innovation was part of the routine — the photographic record reveals how necessity generated solutions for everything from clotheslines to air shafts to a water purification plant.

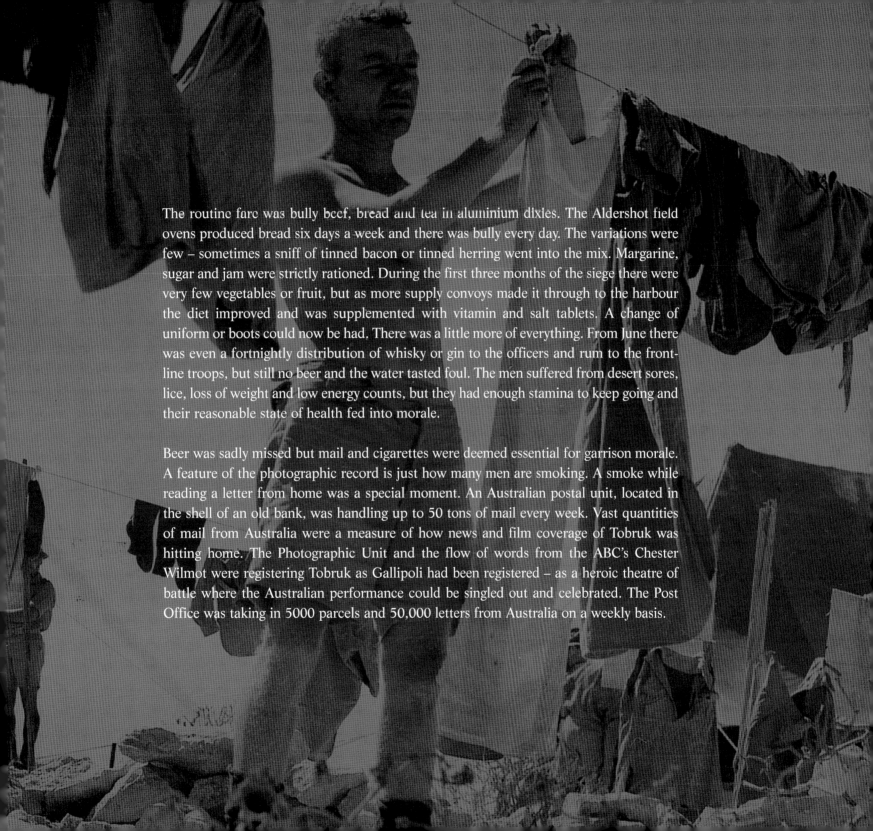

The routine fare was bully beef, bread and tea in aluminium dixies. The Aldershot field ovens produced bread six days a week and there was bully every day. The variations were few – sometimes a sniff of tinned bacon or tinned herring went into the mix. Margarine, sugar and jam were strictly rationed. During the first three months of the siege there were very few vegetables or fruit, but as more supply convoys made it through to the harbour the diet improved and was supplemented with vitamin and salt tablets. A change of uniform or boots could now be had. There was a little more of everything. From June there was even a fortnightly distribution of whisky or gin to the officers and rum to the front-line troops, but still no beer and the water tasted foul. The men suffered from desert sores, lice, loss of weight and low energy counts, but they had enough stamina to keep going and their reasonable state of health fed into morale.

Beer was sadly missed but mail and cigarettes were deemed essential for garrison morale. A feature of the photographic record is just how many men are smoking. A smoke while reading a letter from home was a special moment. An Australian postal unit, located in the shell of an old bank, was handling up to 50 tons of mail every week. Vast quantities of mail from Australia were a measure of how news and film coverage of Tobruk was hitting home. The Photographic Unit and the flow of words from the ABC's Chester Wilmot were registering Tobruk as Gallipoli had been registered – as a heroic theatre of battle where the Australian performance could be singled out and celebrated. The Post Office was taking in 5000 parcels and 50,000 letters from Australia on a weekly basis.

'Ships of the Desert'. On his return to Tobruk in August, stills photographer George Silk came across this unusual dugout. A group of 2/13th Field Engineers had ventilated their living quarters with funnels from a wrecked ship. (George Silk. AWM 009515)

A smoko'. Capt. E. P. Tivey in the officers' quarters at headquarters, 26th Infantry Brigade area. (AWM 020151)

A soldier's photograph of work-mates from the Australian Army Service Corps working on the engine of an AIF truck called 'Joyce'.
(Donated by Pte. J. Dix. AWM P02399.015)

Write as many letters as you can we know our letters off by heart we read them so much.

Pte. R. L. Zuckur, 2/24th Battalion, May 1941

Indian troops preparing a meal in their cookhouse near the front line, September 1941. (AWM 009588)

A cave near 9th Division Headquarters converted into a classroom for signals training. Men came in from the front line for refresher courses, this one on 27 August 1941. (AWM 020300)

Tobruk Truth — the Dinkum Oil came out every day in spite of enemy bombs which once wrecked the office and several times put the radio set or 'printing press' out of action.

Chester Wilmot, *Desert Siege*

The editorial sanctum of the *Tobruk Truth*, better known as the *Dinkum Oil*, 4 May 1941. They carry on in spite of a slight mishap across the street. (Frank Hurley. AWM 007570)

The 'cookhouse' and officers' mess of HQ, 26th Australian Infantry Brigade, April 1941. From left, standing, are Lt. J. D. Linton, Pte. J. Smart, Cpl. Fowler and Driver Smith. The officer seated is unidentified. (AWM 020100)

Dust, flies, fleas, sores. What would we have said had we known we would have been without beer, cigarettes and leave?

Marginal jotting from Damien Parer's notebook

The underground 'Fig Tree' Regimental Aid Post, 30 September 1941. The wounded men on the cave floor are waiting to go to the main dressing station. (AWM 020100)

From a series of 'bakery' photos taken by Frank Hurley on 4 May 1941. These are the Tobruk bakers removing the daily bread from Aldershot ovens in the field. Built of brick and sealed with mud, the ovens were primitive but efficient. They were pre-heated by wood fires. The dough was then placed on the hearths and the ovens sealed. The residual heat of the bricks and stone hearth cooked a batch in about one hour. (Frank Hurley. AWM 007538)

The lookout and the cricketers, but cricket matches were a rare treat. 11 September 1941. (AWM 020790)

Men feel highly strung and feel strain since coming into reserve. Everyone prefers to be in the front line as time hangs too heavy on everyone's hands and it is more annoying not being able to retaliate.

Sergeant C. G. Symington, 2/17th Battalion Diary, 28 April 1943

A game of draughts for the crew of a Bofors 400mm anti-aircraft gun, 17 September 1941. (AWM 020672)

The laundry lines
of the 2/48th
Infantry Battalion,
22 September 1941.
(AWM 020661)

Mass washing. Men
appointed from
each company of
the 2/48th Infantry
Battalion did the
washing for their
unit. Here clothes
are being boiled in
sawn-off 44-gallon
drums doubling as
coppers.
(AWM 020657)

All ranks are undoubtedly jaded, yet to go into a rear area only offers the usual digging tasks with no active patrolling. Some form of amusement is vitally needed to maintain a sense of balance, especially if we are to be here for many more months.

War Diary, 2/13th Battalion, June 1941

Tobruk graffiti. As the evacuation proceeded, Australian soldiers were eager to leave their mark around the town. Here they sign off on the wall of a former café, 20 September 1941. (AWM 020629)

THE 'TOBRUK FERRY SERVICE'

Arrived Tobruk in the dark, unloaded and took on so many wounded, 200 troops and ammunition empties, and proceeded to Mersa Matruh. Air raid at Matruh. Next day embarked ammunition and stores and sailed for Tobruk. Air attacks ...

HMAS Stuart Diarist

The 'Tobruk Ferry Service' was one of the nicknames for the navy and merchant ships that supplied the fortress during the siege. Another name was the 'spud run'. The forces holding Tobruk needed food, weapons, ammunition, petrol, oil, medical and maintenance supplies and much else. They also needed goods that bolstered morale – cigarettes, the mail and the occasional stash of beer. The inward run brought replacements; the outward run took the wounded and the sick.

Replenishing Tobruk was the work of British and Australian navy destroyers, merchant ships and smaller vessels that braved the run from the Egyptian ports of Mersa Matruh and Alexandria. The Ferry Service was a continuous shuttle that might have been dreary had it not been so dangerous. In April about 50 per cent of the convoys were forced to turn back by enemy bombers. Not even the cover of night was a sure thing as the German pilots learnt to pick the ships' moonlit wakes. The last part of the run, as the convoys neared Tobruk Harbour, was called 'bomb alley'.

Chester Wilmot returned to Tobruk early in August on HMS *Decoy* and wrote an account of a nighttime attack on his convoy:

Then above the roar of the engines, wind and sea, from the rear gun-platform an officer shouts through a megaphone: 'Stand by. Action stations.' We wait again. Then, 'Stand by, Enemy aircraft.' Suddenly we're snatching at the nearest rail or bulkhead as the destroyer heels over in a wild zigzag and seems to leap forward. On the slippery deck the cargo slides crashing into the scuppers and the spray drenches everything. Above the turmoil that voice again, 'Stand by. Blitz barrage.' Behind us a great white swathe of wash is even more tell-tale than before … I look across at Havock *[another destroyer in the convoy] – a great stream of black smoke is pouring from her funnels. Then we hear the bomber's drone and* Havock's *guns stab the darkness with red flashes. She rolls over in a 90 degree turn and a hundred yards or so ahead of her a great white water-spout tells us that the Stuka has missed its mark. Out of the darkness ahead we see two pinpoints of light, the harbour lights of Tobruk, shielded from the air but visible to us. We slacken speed. There is no wash now, and a welcome cloud cloaks the moon and other bombers cannot see us. But they are over Tobruk and are going for the harbour. We can hear the muffled crack of the ack-ack guns and see the flashes of bursting shells high in the sky. We slip in between the lights, past the black ghosts of wrecks, under the lee of the white sepulchre of a town.*

(Chester Wilmot, *Desert Siege*)

From a series of
stills taken by
George Silk,
documenting an
HMAS *Perth*
patrol in the
Mediterranean,
1941. After his
photographic shoot
on *Perth*, Silk
returned to
Alexandria, took a
ship to Greece to
cover Allied action
there, then moved
on to Syria and after
that returned to
Tobruk, in August.
His movements are
typical of the
mobility of the
official
photographers.
(George Silk.
AWM 006604)

An issue was made of one orange per man, the first issue of fresh fruit in Tobruk ...

Diarist, 18th Brigade

Anti-aircraft gunners go through their routines on the trip from Alexandria to Tobruk. (AWM 040581)

On a supply ship running the gauntlet between Alexandria and Tobruk. (AWM 040580)

LEFT: An informal portrait of Lt. Alfred (Pedlar) Palmer DSC, Royal Navy Reserve, captain of the Italian schooner HMS *Maria Giovanna*. Lt. Palmer delivered food and supplies to Tobruk weekly between May and November 1941. He navigated by setting course for the direction of the headlights of German lorries on the coast road until he sighted the shaded green light that marked the entrance to Tobruk Harbour. To stop him, the Germans placed a decoy light along the coast and the ship ran ashore. After eight hours resistance, Palmer was captured. During his time as a prisoner he attempted several escapes and on 10 October 1943 he was shot in the arm while trying to escape from a train. The arm was amputated. He was repatriated to England in September 1944. This photo was taken in Tobruk Harbour on 11 September 1941. (AWM 020804)

*Row of men's faces asleep,
camera pans to their feet
which are all on the railing
followed by the same shot
taken from above.*

Damien Parer, October 1941

Mediterranean Sea, 1941. Troops bunked down on the top deck of the destroyer HMAS *Vendetta* on one of her voyages to Tobruk. The supply of Tobruk was largely maintained by destroyers of the Royal Australian Navy's Inshore Squadron under Capt. Hector Waller. *Vendetta, Waterhen, Voyager, Vampire* and *Stuart* operated in a shuttle service between Tobruk and ports in Egypt. As they were all built in 1917-18 they were dubbed the 'ancient warriors'. *Vendetta* made the voyage thirty-nine times between May and August 1941.

(Donor A. Luly. AWM P01810.002)

Suddenly we're snatching at the nearest rail or bulkhead as the destroyer heels over in a wild zigzag and seems to leap forward. On the slippery deck the cargo slides crashing into the scuppers and the spray drenches everything.

Chester Wilmot, August 1941

TOP: Mediterranean Sea, 29 June 1941. A sailor's shot of the destroyer HMAS *Waterhen* in trouble after being attacked and crippled by German divebombers off the port of Salum in Egypt. The crew and troop reinforcements bound for Tobruk are preparing to board the British destroyer HMS *Defender* (not in view), which is about to pull alongside. (Donor A. Luly. AWM P01810.005)

BOTTOM: The next day, 30 June 1941. HMAS *Waterhen* about to roll over and sink. The entire crew and troops were rescued by *Defender.* (Donor A. Luly. AWM P01810.004)

Mediterranean Sea, 11 July 1941. The view from HMAS *Vendetta*. Rescued crew and troops watch the British destroyer HMS *Defender* sinking, about eleven kilometres north of the Egyptian coastal town of Sidi Barrani. *Defender* was on the home run, evacuating troops from Tobruk. (Donor A. Luly. AWM P01810.007)

Time to get the camera. A sailor's shot of men on HMAS *Vendetta* watching
the destroyer HMS *Defender* going down, 11 July 1941. (AWM P00090.041)

On 25 May, the Helka carrying 1,000 tons of bulk petrol for the garrison was sunk about 30 miles north-east of Tobruk.

Barton Maugham, *Tobruk and El Alamein*

The British sloop HMS *Grimsby* (left) listing in the water and a tanker, probably the *Helka*, sinking at right. The ships had been attacked and severely damaged by German aircraft not far from the besieged port of Tobruk. The photograph was taken from the deck of an unidentified ship, 25 May 1941. (Donor A. Luly. AWM P01810.008)

SHOOTING THE WAR

If you are able to describe accurately and graphically the actions in which the troops take part, you must see the ground over which they have to fight.

Chester Wilmot

Winning hearts and minds and maintaining morale on the home front was part of the battle. The Department of Information's Photographic Unit and the ABC's Broadcast Unit were with the Australians during the Western Desert Offensive and the siege.

These were the storytellers, the cinematographers, photographers and journalists who connected the battlefront with the home front. They were constantly moving in pursuit of another story, sometimes acting on no more than rumours or whispers of action, often taking risks as great as any front-line soldier. On many occasions the Photographic team split up leaving a 'one-man band' to cover an impossible amount of ground. While Frank Hurley returned to Tobruk in April, Damien Parer, Ron Williams and George Silk went to Greece, then Syria. Wilmot was with the Western Desert Force in January 1941, then he went on to Greece and Syria. He returned to Tobruk in August, in time to link up with Parer again. They came in from Alexandria with the same convoy but on separate ships. Silk was also back in Tobruk at this time. Whereas most Australian soldiers braved the ocean 'run' in and out of Tobruk only once – on their way out – the newsmen braved it as many times as was required. Some of Parer's best photographs were taken while under attack at sea.

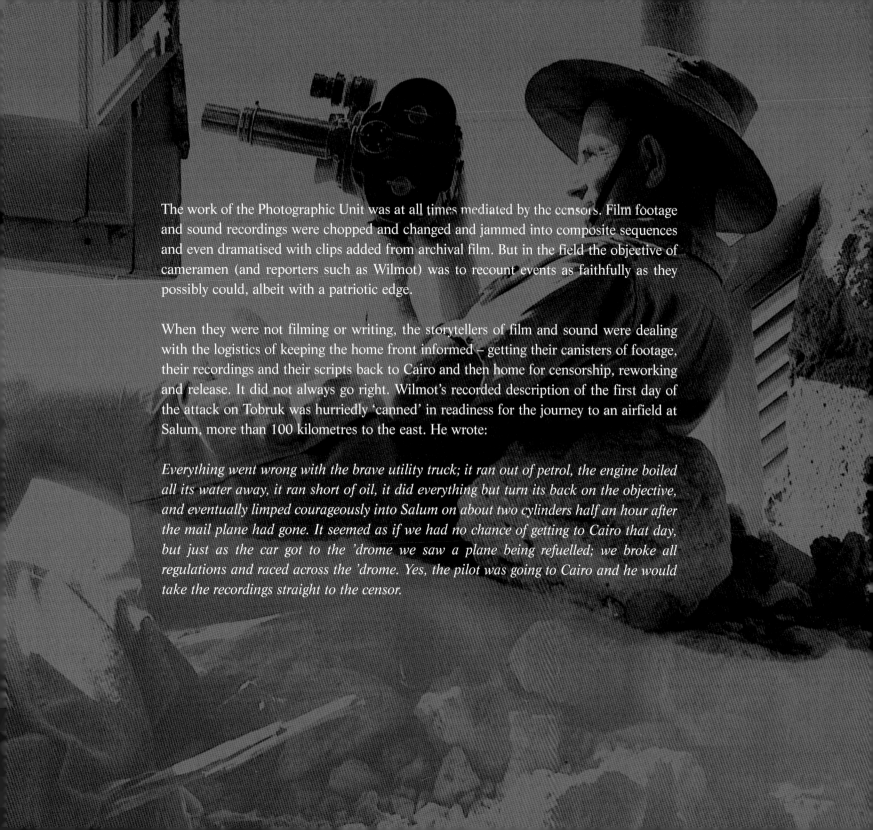

The work of the Photographic Unit was at all times mediated by the censors. Film footage and sound recordings were chopped and changed and jammed into composite sequences and even dramatised with clips added from archival film. But in the field the objective of cameramen (and reporters such as Wilmot) was to recount events as faithfully as they possibly could, albeit with a patriotic edge.

When they were not filming or writing, the storytellers of film and sound were dealing with the logistics of keeping the home front informed – getting their canisters of footage, their recordings and their scripts back to Cairo and then home for censorship, reworking and release. It did not always go right. Wilmot's recorded description of the first day of the attack on Tobruk was hurriedly 'canned' in readiness for the journey to an airfield at Salum, more than 100 kilometres to the east. He wrote:

Everything went wrong with the brave utility truck; it ran out of petrol, the engine boiled all its water away, it ran short of oil, it did everything but turn its back on the objective, and eventually limped courageously into Salum on about two cylinders half an hour after the mail plane had gone. It seemed as if we had no chance of getting to Cairo that day, but just as the car got to the 'drome we saw a plane being refuelled; we broke all regulations and raced across the 'drome. Yes, the pilot was going to Cairo and he would take the recordings straight to the censor.

Three members of the Department of Information's Photographic Unit after Western Desert forces had overwhelmed the Italian garrison at Sidi Barrani, December 1940. From left: Pambo Morrison (driver), Frank Hurley and Alan Anderson. Further on in the offensive they were joined by George Silk and Damien Parer, then the team split again in order to provide a visual record of the war in Greece and Syria, and in the besieged fortress of Tobruk. A small number of photo-graphers and film cameramen covering many theatres was the pattern for the rest of the war. (Frank Hurley. AWM 004461)

Shells flew over the tops of the troops and landed uncomfortably close to Damien and me. So we hopped into the nearest trench, which happened to be an excreta collector for the stone fort ... we stayed there for a while until things eased off and then we trotted over to the panel van to put all the equipment away.

Alan Anderson, Soundman with the Film Unit

George Silk (left) and Damien Parer in the Western Desert, 1941. Silk has the remote control in his hidden hands. (Courtesy Neil McDonald. Basil Butler Collection. Photographer George Silk, reproduced from Parer's own print.)

Back from the front. Damien Parer with cans of film in Cairo, *c*. February 1941. Parer served in Libya and the Middle East, Greece and the South-West Pacific from 1940 until his resignation in May 1943. He was killed on 17 September 1944 while filming front-line operations with the US Marine Corps on Peleliu Island.

(Donor R. Hemmons. Photo by Robert J. Bevir. AWM P02126.014)

RIGHT: Damien Parer (right) with his driver, February 1941. He was between assignments having covered the assault on Derna, then returned to Cairo to prepare for the visit of Sir Robert Menzies that would include a quick tour of Tobruk. Hurley covered the PM's visit on film, Parer took the stills.

(Donor R. Hemmons. Photo by Robert J. Bevir. AWM P02126.013)

Arriving in Cairo from Tobruk I met Ronnie. We went to Palestine to photograph an inspection and went to Haifa for a rest. Of all places in Syria and Palestine I like Haifa the best.

Damien Parer, October 1941. From p. 153 of *Damien Parer's War*

Waiting for a Stuka attack. Damien Parer and George Silk in a bunker on Tobruk Harbour, August 1941. (AWM 009499)

Damien Parer at work with his Newman-Sinclair 35mm camera during the siege of Tobruk, August 1941. The moving footage that he shot was fashioned into eight-minute newsreels for cinemagoers back in Australia and used in the Department of Information's propaganda offensive against pessimism and apathy on the home front. Tobruk was the most powerful story available. (George Silk. AWM 009508)

Streets of Tobruk. The Photographic Unit resting in a bomb crater, 23 January 1941. Present in
the crater are (from left) Pambo Morrison, Alan Anderson and Damien Parer. The church
tower in the background would survive the entire siege. (Frank Hurley. AWM 005411)

Filming with the Cine camera from the ruins of Tobruk, 20 September 1941. Warrant Officer I. T. Fisher of the Military History and Information Section's No.5 Field Unit.
(AWM 020634)

It is of course a terrific show that the garrison has not only held out for seven months but has also hammered the enemy very severely during that time.

Damien Parer to Basil Butler, November 1941

Your ABC. Bill McFarlane, technician with the ABC Unit in Tobruk. (ABC Archives)

A photographer at work outside the office of *Mud and Blood*, the newspaper of the 2/23rd Infantry Battalion, 3 September 1941. (AWM 020511)

August 1941. The dugout used by the Military History and Information Section's 5th Field Unit. Lt. F. A. M. Cade (left) was in charge of the unit and Maj. Howard second in command. (AWM 020225)

GUNNER BRYANT – PHOTO MEMORIES

Merry, oh merry, oh merry, are we,
We are the boys of the artillery,
Sing high, sing low, wherever we go
Artillery gunners we never say no.

British gunners' song from Tobruk

One of the soldier photographers at Tobruk was Gunner R. K. Bryant, who took snaps that included the retreat across the desert, the defence of Tobruk and his eventual evacuation in October. Bryant was a member of 8 Battery, 2/3rd Light Anti-Aircraft Regiment. His unit used a captured Italian Breda gun that was trucked about, first to cover the retreating troops, from Derna eastward, then to defend positions within Tobruk where the truck was dubbed 'Stokes' Travelling Circus' in honour of the regiment's commanding officer, Major Phillip Stokes.

Bryant's photo memories provide a record of a small fighting unit, their camaraderie, their daily routines and the business of war – the care of the gun, the unit in action, the loss of a comrade, the men left behind.

He is in and out of the photographic record because he and his friends took turns to take the pictures. His photographs are typical of soldier photography in a number of ways that are unlike the work of official photographers. Bryant's pictures are a *close-up* of a particular unit, a sequence over time of the experience of ordinary soldiers. They are photos taken for loved ones and friends at home, imbued with a special intimacy, not unlike that of family photos – from the roadside camp to Gunner Buntz sitting on the 'thunderbox' to the photo portrait of Jim Cowie (K.I.A. 25 September 1941) taken not long before his death. Something of the special bond between these men is evident in this photo record, small as it is.

Before the siege of Tobruk. Gnr. Bryant's team at work at Derna Pass, March 1941, soon after the Western Desert Offensive had turned into a full-scale retreat. The men of 8 Battery, 2/3rd Light Anti-Aircraft Regiment, are providing protection for Allied land forces retreating from Benghazi. The team had already begun to specialise in the use of captured Italian guns, this one a 20/65 Breda 20mm Cannon. Left to right: Gnr. R. V. Ince, Gnr. Bryant, Bombadier Roberts, Gnr. Buntz. (Lent by R. K. Bryant. AWM P01260.004)

A not so private moment, June 1941.
Gnr. Buntz on the portable latrine known
as the 'thunderbox'. (Lent by R. K. Bryant.
AWM P01260.013)

RIGHT: In the mess hall of the desert, Tobruk,
June 1941. Men of 8 Battery, 2/3rd Light
Anti-Aircraft Regiment, from left to right:
Gnr. R. V. Ince, Bombadier P. Roberts, Gnr.
R. K. Bryant, a British driver and Gnr. J.
Buntz. The photo was probably taken by one
of the two team members who are not in this
picture – Gnr. J. W. Cowie or Gnr. Jim Croft.
(Lent by R. K. Bryant. AWM P01260.010)

While the official photographers could get extra film on their forays to and from Alexandria, the soldier-photographers were unable to get any film at all. They could use only what film they had when they came into Tobruk. That meant *shots* were rationed. It meant Gnr. Bryant rarely took a photo of an artillery team other than his own for he was documenting *his* war. This photo is an exception – a shot of a 'Bush battery', men of the 2/12th Regiment in action with a captured Italian field gun. (Lent by R. K. Bryant. AWM P01260.008)

Several guns were blown up when shells exploded in the barrel; and after this many pieces of Bush Artillery were fired with the aid of a length of rope by remote control.

Chester Wilmot, *Desert Siege*

After the fall of Greece and Crete the defenders at Tobruk were expecting an airborne invasion. Every man in the gun crews was issued with a rifle and bayonet. Some of these were captured Italian weapons. 8 Battery was issued with .303 Lee Enfields. From left to right: Gnr. R. V. Ince, Gnr. Jim Cowie, Gnr. Bryant and Gnr. Buntz. (Lent by R. K. Bryant. AWM P01260.009)

Back to work. The gun crew in action, June 1941. (Lent by R. K. Bryant. AWM P01260.014)

Tobruk, April 1941. The men of 8 Battery preparing a site for a 20/65 Breda 20mm Cannon. Gnr. Bryant probably took the photo. Left to right: Bombardier P. Roberts, Gnr. J. W. Croft, Gnr. R. V. Ince and Gnr. J. Buntz.

(Lent by R. K. Bryant. AWM P01260.007)

The guns had no sights but we got direction by squinting down the barrel, and range by trial and error.

Sergeant E. D. Rule, 2/28th Battalion

Gnr. Croft hanging out his washing, June 1941. The washing was apparently kept low to avoid drawing enemy shellfire. (Lent by R. K. Bryant. AWM P01260.012)

Gnr. Jim Cowie with 'Stokes' Travelling Circus', May 1941. Killed in action, 25 September 1941.

(Lent by R. K. Bryant. AWM P01260.016)

Gnr. Bryant's team was frequently on the move to provide anti-aircraft cover for artillery batteries and troop deployments. Transport for the men and their Breda guns was an old Chevrolet truck named 'Stokes' Travelling Circus' after their commanding officer, Maj. Phillip Stokes. This photo was taken in April 1941 at the beginning of the long siege. (Lent by R. K. Bryant. AWM P01260.015)

The Tobruk gunners adopted all kinds of subterfuge to hide their guns. Sometimes they fired through a dust screen raised by trucks driven up and down in front of their gun pits.

Chester Wilmot, *Desert Siege*

At sea, departing Tobruk, September 1941. Members of 8 Battery, 2/3rd Light Anti-Aircraft Regiment, on the deck of British destroyer HMS *Griffin* bound for Alexandria.

(Lent by R. K. Bryant. AWM P01260.017)

LAST OUT –
2/13TH
BATTALION

I have learnt a lot in the 9 months in this hell.

Sergeant C. L. Craig, 2/13th Battalion, 29 December 1941

Casualties from all causes were mounting – the strain of the siege was taking a heavy toll on the Australians. In July the Australian Government decided that AIF units at Tobruk must be relieved. The debacle in Greece had effectively wrecked the 6th Division for months to come and the government did not want another division sidelined by death and weariness. The British Government resisted, in part because the evacuation of so many Australians and their replacement in the fortress seemed to be an immensely dangerous and difficult task. But agreement followed. The Australians were evacuated in a series of convoys over a three-month period. In August the 18th Brigade was brought out by sea to rejoin the 7th Division in Syria. The 9th Division units followed in September and October, simultaneously replaced by incoming British and Polish troops.

Night after night the changeover continued. The ships slipped into the harbour. Destroyers berthed alongside half-sunken hulks now operating as wharves. Cruisers unloaded in mid-harbour using the barges. The gunners were ready, constantly watching the skies for enemy bombers. The work was feverish. In about half an hour 1000 men had disembarked and hundreds of tons of stores were unloaded. Then the Australians streamed onboard, their packs and haversacks bulging with souvenirs crafted from shell-cases, grenades and fragments of wrecked planes. Holds closed, rope ladders came up, lines were cast off and the convoy steamed out of the harbour into the night.

The last of the Australians scheduled to leave were the men of the 2/13th Battalion, but their convoy was attacked on the night of 25 October, partly destroyed and forced back to Alexandria. It was almost dawn when the 2/13th learnt that they would not be leaving. The final night of an otherwise successful relief was a total failure.

The men of the 2/13th stayed on at Tobruk as the only Australian presence in the garrison. They were there until 21 November when they took part in a break-out to the east aimed at linking up with 'Operation Crusader', a British thrust from Egypt. At El Duda they captured vital ground in a night bayonet attack that took 167 prisoners at a cost of two killed and five wounded.

The Crusader offensive was a success. Rommel was forced to abandon the area between Tobruk and the Egyptian border and shift his forces to the west of the fortress. On 16 December the 2/13th Battalion moved out by road to rejoin the 9th Division in Palestine. An epic, eight-month siege came to an end.

Well tonight's the night ... Everything is packed and the new mob to relieve us will be up soon. I feel excited and it's impossible to describe the feeling I have inside me for getting out of this place, away from the flies, dust, heat and death and wounds.

Sergeant Cec' Greenwood, 2/17th Battalion,
22 October 1941

Four veterans of Tobruk preparing to disembark at Alexandria, October 1941.
(AWM 021160)

RIGHT: Alexandria, Egypt, 27 September 1941. Members of the anti-aircraft and artillery units waiting to disembark the cruiser that transported them from Tobruk.
(AWM 020457)

Veterans of Tobruk having a meal onboard ship, en route to Alexandria, October 1941.
(AWM 021166)

The spirit of the battalion is still good and the defences of its section of Tobruk are as secure as ever. But a calculating outlook has definitely crept in as regards the 'joie de vivre' of raiding. I expect this will grow unless some event takes place to change our outlook.

War Diary, 2/13th Battalion, June 1941

In Australia, by sticking together men have defied drought, bush-fire and flood. In Tobruk they've scorned hardship, danger and death, because no Digger would ever let his cobbers down. In Tobruk for the first time in this war the Germans were thrust back by a spirit that even tanks and dive-bombers could not conquer.

Chester Wilmot, dialogue for film sequence shot by Damien Parer

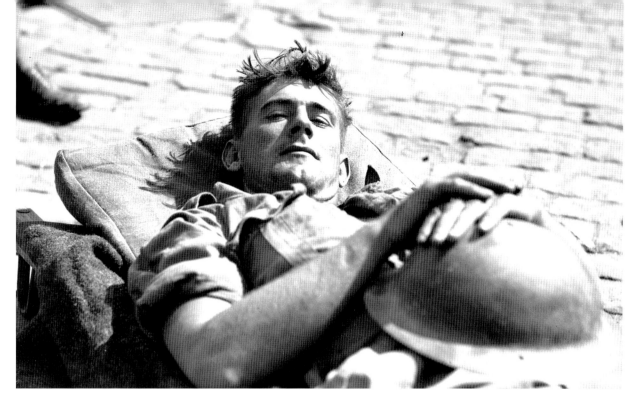

A wounded Australian on the dock at Alexandria after the journey from Tobruk, 27 September 1941. (AWM 020469)

Stretcher cases en route to ambulances. Alexandria, 27 September 1941. (AWM 020465)

LEFT: 9th Division veterans of the siege of Tobruk disembarking at Alexandria, October 1941. (AWM 021159)

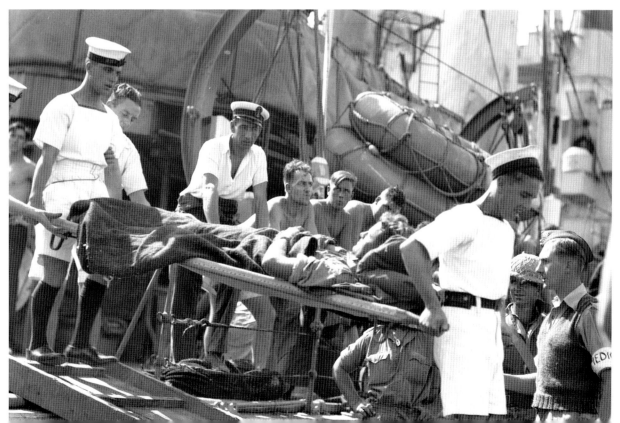

Back on dry land. Men of the 24th Infantry Brigade at Alexandria, 27 September 1941. (AWM 020461)

After we took the position we were shelled continuously for two days. Had we not been relieved after the second night I think half the coy. Would have gone shell happy. It was terrible I can't describe it.

Private. A. Armstrong, 2/13th Battalion Diary, December 1941

The Australians left behind – men of the 2/13th Battalion after the relief of Tobruk in December 1941. The 2/13th took part in the break-out and the battle of El Duda. Damien Parer, George Silk and Chester Wilmot covered some of the fighting. The men here are, from left: Pte. L. E. Everett, Pte. A. O'Connor, Pte G. Richardson and Pte. J. W. Cox. (Damien Parer. AWM 010979)

As Australian soldiers prepared to leave Tobruk, one of the final rituals was a visit to the graves of mates killed in action during the siege. Some with cameras took photographs of graves for families at home. These men, at the cemetery on 16 October, were among the last Australians to depart by sea. (AWM 020990)

The 2/13th Battalion was to leave Tobruk on 25 October. In the weeks preceding, the men of the 2/13th put finishing touches to the graves of lost companions.
(AWM 020989)

I left a few men in Libya in their last resting places and I managed to visit the cemetery before I left. I never spent a more miserable hour I can assure you and it was hard to leave them there – but I know that they shall ever be remembered.

Lieutenant L. H. Heffron, 2/48th Battalion,
12 November 1941

A soldier's photograph of the Australian cemetery at Tobruk. Bare earth, rough stone and wooden crosses. The boundary in the distance is a line of 44-gallon drums. The stone cart in the centre suggests unfinished work. 832 Australians died in the siege of Tobruk.
(Donor J. Dix. AWM P02399.021)

The cemetery with a newly erected memorial in the background, 9 October 1941. (AWM 020895)

PORTRAITS

In the years between World War I and World War II, photo portraiture for young professionals like Damien Parer, George Silk and others became a more spontaneous and instinctive craft. Gone, or at least demoted, was the preference for the carefully composed shot, the formal square-on angle, the respectful distance between camera and subject. The 'New Photography' as it was called was more intrusive and revealing and this soon showed in photographs of Australia's Diggers at war.

The New Photography was characterised by the close-up and the bird's-eye view. It embraced all the angles. Smaller, more proficient cameras seemed to have liberated the photographer and freed up vision as never before. The 'stolen' moment or the 'captured' expression was now valued as much as the constructed, formal pose, which still had its place in soldier portraiture.

Film was an important influence too. In the single frame taken from movie footage, photographers saw new opportunities for stills. Images became more like fragments from a sequence and some camera angles seemed to enhance possibilities for heroic imagery that European filmmakers had explored in the 1920s and 1930s. Inspired by the doyen in Sydney, Max Dupain, some of the best young Australian photographers had absorbed these influences before the war began, and in photo portraiture from Tobruk we see these influences at work.

On the one hand there are the photo portraits that seem so spontaneous, a chance image frozen in time – Sergeant Souter tucking into his bread and jam, eying the camera suspiciously. On the other hand there are the low-angle shots of the gunners, carefully posed to convey the virility and heroic force of the defenders at Tobruk. The composition is statuesque. These men might have been carved from stone. It is the perspective we have when we look up at a warrior statue. Damien Parer, George Silk and possibly other photographers at Tobruk took war photography to a new level – close-ups provided the intimacy and the emotions of the captured moment. They also took portraits of men that seemed to embody triumph. As Churchill put it when he wrote to the defenders of Tobruk: 'The whole empire is watching'.

The damaged pipe. George Silk caught a cheerful Pte. C. Howley as he left the front line for a spell, sometime in August 1941. Howley had been on the outer perimeter for ten days. (George Silk. AWM 009512)

Waiting for something to happen. Pte. J. Collins photographed in one of the front-line positions. (AWM 009523)

Heroic portraiture. Defenders of Tobruk ready to ward off Nazi planes. (AWM 040608)

Sighting an anti-tank gun, 11 September 1941. (AWM 020799)

LEFT: Gnr. Jeff Coombe of Launceston (Tasmania), 3rd Anti-Tank Regiment, 9th Division. (AWM 020723)

The low-angle shot again. A gunner from 8 Battery, 3rd Light Anti-Aircraft Regiment in ready-for-action pose. (AWM 020567)

Goggles versus sandstorms. An Australian soldier in a forward section of the front line, 30 August 1941. (AWM 020486)

The use of shadows. An informal portrait reminiscent of some of Max Dupain's photos. Lt. Alf (Pedlar) Palmer on the deck of the Tobruk supply ship, HMS *Maria Giovanna*. (AWM 020797)

Bombadier E. J. Courtney, 8 Battery, 3rd Light Anti-Aircraft Regiment, 11 September 1941. Courtney was awarded the Military Medal for bravery and devotion to duty under the heavy dive-bombing attacks of 25 April to 7 May 1941.
(AWM 020801)

Fisherman, Tobruk Harbour, 25 September 1941. Bill Woodhouse of Wynnum, Brisbane, with his catch. The Australians varied their ration with fish caught in their spare time. On this occasion the stunning technique was used – a stick of gelignite.
(AWM 020635)

Driver Frank Clough of Newcastle (England), a member of the Royal Tank Regiment, photographed on 4 October 1941.
(AWM 021059)

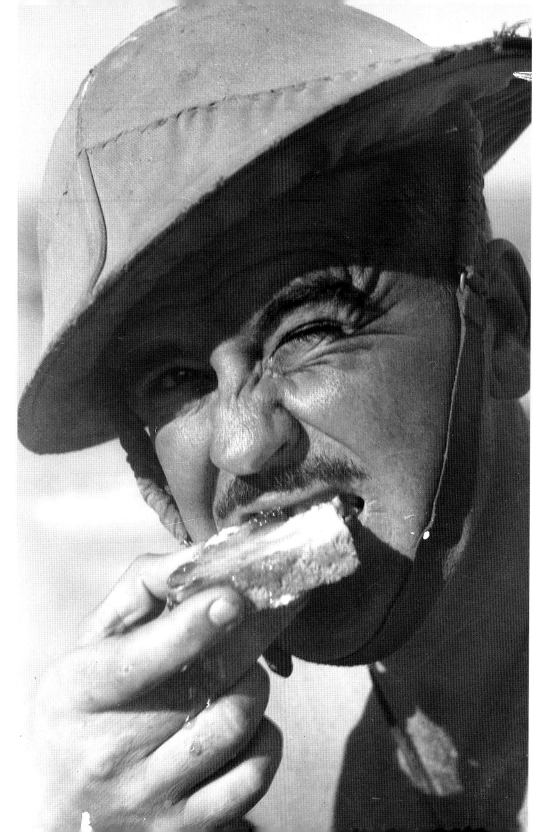

The end of a long patrol, 25 September 1941. Sgt. Bill Souter of Sydney makes short work of his slice of bread and jam. (AWM 020637)

ACKNOWLEDGEMENTS

Special thanks to my commissioning editor Jill Brown, to managing editor Brigitta Doyle, to designer Melanie Feddersen and to photos editor Linda Brainwood. I must also thank Mignon Turpin for her thorough and constructive editing work on the text and Penny Mansley for a fine proofreading job. In the course of researching *Tobruk* I received valuable advice on both the military and photography themes from Neil McDonald, Garth Pratten, Suzanne Rickard and Peter Stanley. Thanks to all for their generosity with helpful comments and criticism.

PRINCIPAL SOURCES

Chris Coulthard-Clark, *Where the Australians Fought. The Encyclopaedia of Australia's Battles*, Allen & Unwin, Sydney, 1988.

Mark Johnston, *That Magnificent 9th. An Illustrated History of the 9th Division 1940-46*, Allen & Unwin, Sydney, 2002.

Gavin Long, *To Benghazi*, Collins/Australian War Memorial, Canberra, 1986 (first published 1952).

Neil McDonald, *Damien Parer's War*, Lothian Books, South Melbourne, 2004. First published as *War Cameraman. The Story of Damien Parer* (1994).

Neil McDonald, *Chester Wilmot Reports*, ABC Books, Sydney, 2004.

Barton Maugham, *Tobruk and El Alamein*, Collins/Australian War Memorial, Canberra, 1987 (first published 1966).

Chester Wilmot, *Desert Siege*, (Australian War Classics volume), Penguin, Camberwell, 2003. First published as *Tobruk 1941*, Angus & Robertson, Sydney, 1944.

MAROUBRA. S
A.G
KILLARNEY
Q L
J BRAHAM
VX2167
CARLTON
SX. 8509
R.L. BOYES
2/48th
ADELAIDE
ROBINSON
TOOWOOMBA
Q.L.D